THE CHILDREN'S FRIENDS

PRIMARY PRESIDENTS AND THEIR LIVES OF SERVICE

JANET PETERSON AND LaRENE GAUNT

DESERET BOOK COMPANY
SALT LAKE CITY, UTAH

To Dr. Thomas J. Parmley, a friend of Primary,
and to our Primary children, past and future

Janet Peterson

To Primary workers throughout the Church.
May the examples of these great leaders
of children inspire you in your callings.

LaRene Gaunt

ON THE COVER: Patricia Peterson Pinegar, currently serving as
Primary general president, loves spending time with children.

Photographs of the Primary presidents on pages xiv, 24, 40, 58, 78, 102,
120, 140, and 166 courtesy of the Historical Department Archives of The
Church of Jesus Christ of Latter-day Saints. Used by permission.

ISBN 1-57345-020-0

Printed in the United States of America

10 9 8 7 6 5 4 3 2 1

Contents

Acknowledgments

We wish to thank our editors at Deseret Book Company, Eleanor Knowles and Linda Gundry, for their gracious and expert help in preparing this manuscript for publication, and the staff of the Church Historical Library and Church Archives for giving us access to historical documents.

Families of the Primary general presidents, counselors in the general presidencies, secretaries, and general board members have willingly shared their memories, insights, and materials. Trilba J. Lindsay has been particularly generous in helping us with this project. Spending an hour with President Gordon B. Hinckley as he reminisced about his childhood and his stepmother was the highlight of our experience.

We especially thank Linda Lamborn, Bud Keysor, Barbara H. Moench, Lorin L. Moench, Carol H. Cannon, Ramona H. Sullivan, Sherman B. Hinckley, Joan W. Peterson, Thomas J. Parmley, Frances P. Muir, Richard T. Parmley, William W. Parmley, Nick Watts, Stan Watts, June W. Jensen, Beryl W. Neff, Vickie M. Stewart, Roden G. Shumway, Jan S. Christensen, Shari S. Oman, Roger G. Shumway, A. Vard Maxfield, Leah M. Sims, Thomas Young, Vauna S. Jacobsen, Alan Jacobsen, Michael Young, Paul Young, Christine Y. Knudson, Suzanne Y. Jones, Jeffrey Young, Leonard M Grassli, Jane Anne G. Woodhead, Susan G. Anderson, Sara G. Chugg, Dean S. Packer, Dottie M. Packer, Deanne P. Kelly, Richard M. Packer,

Kelly M. Packer, Ed J. Pinegar, Karie P. Bushnell, Steven Pinegar, Kelly P. Hagemeyer, Kristi P. Gubler, Brett Pinegar, Traci P. Magleby, Tricia Pinegar, Laurence Peterson, David Peterson, Larry Peterson, and Laurelee P. Passey.

Our families have once again supported us and shared our enthusiasm in researching and writing about the general auxiliary presidents. We give love and appreciation to our husbands, Larry Peterson and David Gaunt; and to our children, Scott, Tom, Gregory, Jeffrey, and Brent Peterson; David and Stephanie P. Bywater; and Angela, Dennis, and Lisa Gaunt.

Introduction

"What is best for the child?" has been the query of all the sisters who have served as general presidents of the Primary. With loving and inspired concern and care, these great women have sought to better the lives of children throughout the world. Their contributions have included suggesting an organization within the Church specifically for children, publishing a children's magazine, funding a children's hospital, implementing modern teaching techniques in the Primary classroom setting, focusing on children's needs and welfare, and most of all, teaching children the gospel of Jesus Christ.

Not all of the Primary presidents had children of their own, but each of them has loved children and has spent her time and energies seeking to better children's lives not only in Church settings but also in any other settings in which she can assist parents and other adults as nurturers and teachers of children.

The lessons of love, nurturing, sacrifice, and testimony taught by the Primary general presidents are timeless and beneficial. The old African tribal proverb "It takes a village to raise a child" reminds us that we each have a significant role in the lives of children around us whether we are mothers, fathers, grandparents, teachers, leaders, relatives, or neighbors. We, too, need to ask the question, "What is best for the child?" and then act upon the answers we receive.

The Primary Association of The Church of Jesus Christ of Latter-day Saints developed because of the concern of adults for the welfare of children.

With the arrival of the first Saints in the Salt Lake Valley in 1847, the widening circle of settlements from that hub, and the continuing flood of emigrant converts, mostly from Europe, community life had become well established in the Territory of Utah by the 1870s. Farming was the primary occupation of most families, with labor divided among family members. Although the Utah Territorial Legislature created school districts in 1851, education was neither free nor available for all children. (Tax-supported education would not be funded until the 1890s.) Thus, parents who were able sent their children to either private or ward schools. The Church was the focal point of the various communities as well as for Latter-day Saint families.

In 1869, Brigham Young organized his daughters into an association known as the Young Ladies Department of the Cooperative Retrenchment Association. Soon its name was shortened to the Retrenchment Association, and similar groups were organized in various communities for young women. By 1875, the Young Men's Mutual Improvement Association was formed, and the organization for the young women (which became the Young Ladies' Mutual Improvement Association), along with the organization for young men, provided spiritual instruction, lessons on self-improvement, and activities for youth fourteen and older. But there was not yet an organization for children.

Because of the necessity of fathers and older sons farming long hours and mothers and older daughters keeping the household with its myriad tasks functioning, younger children often had much unsupervised leisure time. Parents, teachers, and local leaders worried about the unruliness and mischievous behavior of children. One woman who sought to modify behavior of children was Louisa Free Wells, wife of Salt Lake City Mayor Daniel H. Wells. She formed a manners school, known as "Aunt Louisa's Manner Meeting," to teach Daniel's large family lessons on manners, proper speech, prayer, and honesty.[1]

When President Brigham Young visited Farmington, a community located fifteen miles north of Salt Lake City, to organize the Davis Stake in 1877, he said, "We expect to see a radical change, a reformation in the midst of this people."[2] John W. Hess, bishop of the Farmington Ward, responding to President Young's encouragement, turned his attention to the children, particularly the boys, in his ward. He called the mothers in the ward together and explained his concerns to them. He also planned to meet with the fathers at another time.

Aurelia Spencer Rogers listened attentively and over the next several months pondered what might be done for the children. She recorded: "I was always an earnest thinker, and naturally of a religious turn of mind. And for some time previous to the organization of the children I had reflected seriously upon the necessity of more strict discipline for our little boys.

"Many of them were allowed to be out late at night; and certainly some of the larger ones well deserved the undesirable name of 'hoodlum.'"[3]

When Eliza R. Snow, president of the Relief Society, and Emmeline B. Wells, editor of the *Woman's Exponent,* visited Farmington in March 1878, Aurelia expressed her feelings and presented a plan. "What will our girls do for good husbands, if this state of things continues? . . . Could there not be an organization for little boys, and have them trained to make better men?"[4]

Eliza conveyed Aurelia's idea to President John Taylor, Brigham Young's successor as president of the Church. He subsequently wrote to Bishop Hess authorizing him to organize the children in his ward into an association expressly for them. Bishop Hess called Aurelia to preside over this new ward children's organization. Although at first her main concern had been for the improved behavior of the boys, she felt that "the meeting would not be complete without [girls]; for as singing was necessary, it needed the voices of little girls as well as boys to make it sound as well as it should."[5]

Aurelia received an affirmation from the Lord that this new cause in which she was engaged was pleasing. She wrote: "While thinking over what was to be done for the best good of the children, I seemed to be carried away in the spirit, or at least I experienced a feeling of untold happiness which lasted three days and nights. During that time nothing could worry or irritate me; if my little ones were fretful, or the work went wrong, I had patience, could control in kindness, and manage my household affairs easily. This was a testimony to me that what was being done was from God."[6]

The Farmington Ward Primary Association was formally organized on August 11, 1878. Aurelia Spencer Rogers was sustained as the president, with Louisa Haight and Helen M. Miller as her counselors, Rhoda Richards as secretary, and Sara Richards as assistant secretary. Later, Clara H. Leonard was named as treasurer.

Two weeks later, the first Primary meeting was held on Sunday, August 25, in the rock chapel in Farmington. Of the 224 children in the ward, 215 children from the ages of six to fourteen attended. Aurelia felt that this first meeting was "not quite a success on account of unforeseen hindrances and some of the children not knowing the hour of meeting."[7] The weekly meetings were held on Saturday afternoons. Children were taught lessons on faith, obedience, prayer, punctuality, and manners (specifically, the boys were encouraged to not take fruit from orchards and melon patches, and the girls were exhorted not to hang on wagons).[8] Music became an integral part of the program, as did recitations, gardening projects, annual fairs, and lessons in home arts.

Eliza Snow had proposed as the organization's name the Primary Mutual Improvement Association of The Church of Jesus Christ of Latter-day Saints. *Mutual Improvement* was soon dropped, and the organization was most often simply called Primary.

On June 19, 1880, President John Taylor organized separate general presidencies for the Relief Society, Young Ladies Mutual Improvement Association, and the Primary Association. Louie Bouton Felt was called as the first Primary general president, with Matilda W. Barratt and Clara C. M. Cannon as her counselors. She presided over the Primary for forty-five years, until her death in 1925.

Eight other women have served as general presidents of the Primary:

May Anderson, 1925–1939

May Green Hinckley, 1940–1943

Adele Cannon Howells, 1943–1951

LaVern Watts Parmley, 1951–1974

Naomi Maxfield Shumway, 1974–1980

Dwan Jacobsen Young, 1980–1988

Michaelene Packer Grassli, 1988–1994

Patricia Peterson Pinegar, 1994–present

These nine women, truly children's friends, have served faithfully and under inspiration from the Lord to improve conditions for children, to provide them with joyful experiences, and to help instill in all Primary children a love for the gospel and strong testimonies of Jesus Christ.

1

Louie Bouton Felt

1880–1925

*L*ouie B. Felt, the first Primary general president, and her counselor May Anderson were walking down a street in Salt Lake City one afternoon and saw a crippled boy having difficulty maneuvering on his crutches. Watching him struggle brought to their minds many other children who were suffering or in need of medical care. Both women felt that the Primary should do something to help. As they continued their walk, they discussed the plight of sick children, especially those whose parents could not afford adequate medical care. They conceived the idea of endowing a room for children at the LDS Hospital. Later, in 1911, when they presented their plan to Church President Joseph F. Smith and the Primary general board, the Brethren and board approved establishing a children's unit at the Groves LDS Hospital—one room for boys and one for girls. Thus began the program that would bless many children and would eventually lead to the founding of the Primary Children's Hospital. This program was one of many accomplishments of Louie Bouton Felt, who served as Primary general president for forty-five years. Although she never had children of her own, her deep love for all children and her intense desire to better their lives was manifest throughout her lengthy administration.

New England Beginnings

Sarah Louise Bouton was born in Norwalk, Connecticut, on May 5, 1850, and was the third of five children of Joseph and Mary Barto Bouton. Throughout her life, she was known as Louie.

Her Huguenot ancestors, the Boutons, were driven from France in the late sixteenth century because of their religious beliefs. The Boutons thus immigrated to England and then to the United States in the early 1600s, arriving in Boston and settling in Connecticut. Louie's great-great-great-grandfather, John Bouton, who was born in Stamford, Connecticut, in 1607, helped found the town of Norwalk, Connecticut, where the Boutons lived for generations.

Louie's parents joined The Church of Jesus Christ of Latter-day Saints several years before her birth. Louie was baptized at age eight in a cove along the Connecticut seashore. Because Joseph Bouton served as the branch president in Norwalk, the family received visits from Church leaders, including Brigham Young, John Taylor, and George Q. Cannon.

The Boutons opened their home to missionaries, often hosting clambakes for them. For such occasions, they invited other branch members, with the women preparing a picnic and all traveling by boats to a small island near the Bouton home, named Nauvoo Island by John Taylor. The men donned bathing suits or old clothes and at low tide dug clams buried in the sand. They cooked the clams in an oven built of rocks. An article in the *Children's Friend* reported that after one clambake, Elder George Q. Cannon realized that he had left his collar and tie on Nauvoo Island. Worried, Louie convinced her brother to take her out to the island early the next morning. She found the collar and tie but was unable to return them to their owner because he had left for New York. She washed and ironed the articles of clothing, and when he visited again, he found them neatly laid out in his room. George asked who had done this kindness, but shy Louie would not own up to it. When he realized it was Louie, he gave the collar and tie to her for a souvenir.[1]

The Boutons spent leisure time together gathering flowers, berries, and nuts and dredging Long Island Sound for clams. She often helped her Grandfather Bouton harvest sap from his grove of maple trees. He built a fire outdoors to boil the maple syrup and let the children taste it when it cooled. According to the *Children's Friend,* "The children ran to him and held out their tin plates to catch the drippings which fell from his paddle. He was such a jolly good natured man that he let the drops form fantastic shapes on their tin plates. After the maple syrup was done, Grandpa Bouton poured it out into large pans and cut it into squares ready for the market."[2] Louie also helped her father and brothers dredge oysters in Long Island Sound and gather nuts in the fall from the abundant trees near their home. Louie enjoyed winter sports, especially ice skating, and became a skilled skater.

Louie's family prepared all Saturday to keep the Sabbath strictly. "On Saturday all of Sunday's food—the meat, the vegetables, and the pudding—was placed in the large bake oven in the basement," according to an account of Louie's childhood. "Paper and wood were arranged so that all that was necessary on Sunday morning was to light the match and adjust the dampers so the fire would not smoke. Louie had special clothes to be worn on Sunday. There was the dress, the underwear, the stockings and shoes, the gloves, hat and wrap which were not worn on any other day. It was in these that she went to Sunday school and [sacrament] meeting to worship the Lord in her quiet way. She was never allowed to sing light songs, nor play games, because Sunday is the Lord's day and it is sacred."[3]

Louie's mother taught her homemaking skills—cooking, mending, dusting, and cleaning. When Louie was quite young, the family's cook taught her to make bread. She was so short she had to stand on a stool in order to knead the bread, but hers turned out so well that she became the family's designated breadmaker. She also learned to make excellent pies.

Louie learned valuable lessons as well as homemaking skills from her mother. One day a group of women who had come to visit Mary started gossiping about a neighbor. Later,

Louie asked her mother why she had left the room. She replied, "Louie dear, they were talking about the personal affairs of people which I have no right to hear, and I did not wish to."[4]

The Trek to Utah

In 1864, when Louie was fourteen, the Boutons left Connecticut to join the Saints in Utah. While they were en route to Omaha, Nebraska, by train, a fire in the baggage car destroyed all their belongings. Discouraged, they returned to Norwalk to begin preparations all over again. Two years later, in May 1866, they started out once more, heading for Omaha by train and by boat. Although their possessions reached Omaha safely this time, Joseph Bouton became seriously ill and could not continue the journey. Joseph, Mary, and two of their children stayed east of Omaha with two missionaries who were traveling with the group, while Louie and her brothers, Harry and Frank, traveled with some missionaries to Omaha. The Bouton family sent a telegram to Church members there requesting that someone meet and house Louie and her brothers until the rest of family arrived.

In Omaha, Joseph H. Felt received the telegram. Recently returned from his mission to England, Denmark, and Sweden, he was in charge of the Saints in Omaha at the time. When he and other single elders read the Boutons' telegram, they vied for the opportunity of meeting the arriving party. Joseph won and met Louie and her traveling companions at the train station.

The Boutons were reunited in Omaha four days later, but Joseph's illness delayed their departure for Utah for another six weeks. Joseph and Louie became friends during this time. Finally, the time came when the family could wait no longer to make the difficult wagon trek without the risk of running into cold and snowy weather. So although Joseph was not well, the family nevertheless joined a wagon company and journeyed to the Salt Lake Valley, arriving on September 19, 1866. Louie's father never regained his health.

Louie's Courtship and Marriage

Joseph Henry Felt had been born in Salem, Massachusetts, in 1840, and baptized at age eleven in 1851, eight years after his parents, Nathaniel Henry and Eliza Ann Preston Felt, had joined the Church. From their first meeting, Joseph was attracted to Louie, with her blue eyes, blonde hair, and tall, slender figure. Once both Joseph and Louie were living in Salt Lake, they saw each other frequently. Twenty-six-year-old Joseph and sixteen-year-old Louie were married December 29, 1866. His parents hosted a wedding celebration at their home, which was attended by Brigham Young and other Church leaders.

At the 1867 October general conference, Brigham Young called the newlyweds to help settle the Muddy River Mission (now Moapa) in southeastern Nevada. On November 9, the young couple, along with several other families, left for St. George. It was a difficult trip, with rivers to ford, quicksand to avoid, and mountains and barely passable roads to traverse. One of Joseph's friends begged him to stay in St. George, describing the harsh conditions along the Muddy River. The Muddy was a three-day journey from St. George, itself a struggling settlement in the desert. Joseph was tempted to stay, for the move had been more difficult than he anticipated, and he feared that Louie, who was not strong, was worn out by the three-hundred-mile trek. The strains of the journey did indeed take their toll on Louie's health: complications from a miscarriage during this time left her permanently unable to have children.

When Joseph asked Louie about staying, however, she immediately replied, "We were not sent to St. George; we were sent to the Muddy. You may do as you please; I am going on."[5] This trait of putting aside health concerns and tenaciously moving ahead would be characteristic of Louie throughout her life.

At the Muddy, the colonists lived in tents and wagons until they could build adobe houses. All the mission families lived inside the fort, while their farms were located outside it. One family, seeing the Felts' situation, gave them their chicken coop as a temporary home.

An even higher priority than housing was planting. Farming in the desert was made more difficult by the sand that filled the irrigation canals during frequent sandstorms. The men labored to deepen and widen the canals, finally overcoming the problem by planting brush along the banks to keep out the sand. Although the canals became usable, growing a successful crop was all but impossible with the wind-driven sand cutting off the young plants and Indians picking the squash and melons as soon as they began to form. Nighttime temperatures during the summer seldom dropped below one hundred degrees.

Joseph began building an adobe home by clearing the site of brush, then making a mold for the adobe bricks and digging a large hole in which to mix the adobe. Louie sewed a pair of bloomers for herself so that she could trample the clay and water with her feet. The Felts' home, though better than the chicken coop, was quite primitive, with a blanket for a door, an adobe floor covered with carpet, a roof made of brush and mud, and muslin coverings stretched over the window openings. Their other furniture consisted of two chairs, a rocker, bed springs laid on top of a storage bin, and a tin wash basin set on top of a packing box. Joseph made a table of brush limbs and boxes.

Through all the difficulties, including a serious shortage of provisions and a fire that nearly destroyed the whole fort, Louie said, "I never felt to murmur, but stay as long as required."[6] Brigham Young visited the settlers in 1869 and, upon seeing their miserable conditions, abandoned the mission. The Felts returned to Salt Lake City, where Joseph went to work at ZCMI.

An Expanding Family

While Louie was living in Nevada, her father's health worsened, and he was advised by Brigham Young to return to his home in Connecticut. Several months later, when Louie visited her parents in Connecticut, she felt she should stay with them, but her ailing father insisted that she return to Utah, stating, "I cannot die in peace until I know you are back with the people of God." Reluctantly, she returned to Salt Lake City and sent a telegram to notify her parents of her safe arrival. Her father said, "Now I can go in peace," and he died that night.[7]

With an inheritance from Louie's father, Louie and Joseph purchased property in Salt Lake City at First South and Seventh East streets. The new home that they constructed on the lot had two rooms and a kitchen, a vast improvement over their adobe house in Nevada.

Louie concluded that plural marriage would provide the ideal resolution to the problem of her childlessness. She wrote, "I became thoroughly convinced of the truth of the principle of celestial marriage and, having no children of my own, was very desirous my husband should take other wives that he might have posterity to do him honor."[8] When she urged him to take her friend Alma Elizabeth (Lizzie) Mineer as a second wife, he was reluctant and told Louie, "I will never love anyone but you, sweetheart." He married Lizzie in 1875, with Louie standing beside them during the wedding ceremony at the Endowment House.[9] Joseph and Lizzie became the parents of three daughters—Louie, Vera, and Etta. Grateful for Lizzie and the girls, Louie wrote, "The Lord gave me a mother's love for them; they seemed as if they were indeed my own, and they seem to have the same love for me as for their own mother."[10] Young Louie became known as "Little Louie." The girls called the two women "Louie Ma" and "Lizzie Ma," and many people did not know which one was the mother of the girls.

Because of increased persecution of polygamous families, Lizzie had to go into hiding, taking only her baby, Etta, with her. Little Louie and Vera stayed with "Louie Ma." During that time, three-year-old Vera contracted diphtheria. Treatment for the disease required putting the patient into a tent of blankets filled with burning lime. Louie stayed with Vera night and day to comfort the young child, who was frightened by the dark, smelly tent.

Louie would often arrange for Lizzie to visit her two daughters; she would hitch a horse to a cart and drive in the

middle of the night to the home where Lizzie was hiding, then
drive a disguised Lizzie back home, hiding the baby in the bottom of the cart.[11]

In 1881, Joseph married a third wife, Elizabeth Liddell.
Both sister wives were given building lots so they could have
their own homes, as Louie did. Joseph, like many other polygamous husbands, lived with each wife for a week or so at a
time. Lizzie Mineer had one more daughter and two sons,
while Elizabeth Liddell had three sons and four daughters. But
over time, relationships changed and Elizabeth divorced
Joseph, sold her lot, and moved to California with her children.

Joseph Felt filled two more missions after his three mar-
riages. In 1883, he served for a year in the Indian Territories,
and then, in 1885, departed for the Eastern States Mission for
two years. It was difficult for his three wives and their children
to have him gone three years out of four. During his absence,
Louie immersed herself in her Primary work and in taking care
of Little Louie and Vera.

All were happy about his return in 1887. A ZCMI
employee from 1869 until he died on June 15, 1907, at the age
of sixty-seven, Joseph traveled quite often for the company,
sometimes working as a "drummer," or traveling salesman.
Prominent in his diaries are notations of work, such as "business good," "business quiet," and "business fair." Very little is
revealed of his family relationships in the diaries, but frequent
mention is made of attending the theater, Sunday School parties, and funerals with Louie and Lizzie and of his wives hosting parties and birthday celebrations. He faithfully listed gifts
received—with the presents Louie gave always outnumbering
anyone else's.

While the second and third wives gave Joseph posterity,
Louie felt they also gave her children. Lillie Freeze, who served
as one of Louie's counselors in the general presidency, remembered that Louie frequently told her friends that plural marriage gave her everything—children and grandchildren.[12]
However, it was against their mother's wishes that Louie raised
Little Louie and Vera as her own. In her home, Little Louie and

Vera enjoyed such advantages as music, dancing, and art lessons. In 1916, Little Louie—now Louie Felt Keysor, the young mother of four children—died unexpectedly. Her children, Elsa, Judith, Alma May, and James Bernard (Bud) Keysor, moved in with Louie and Vera.

Bud Keysor remembered Louie, his guardian, as a "large and beautiful person with a very strong personality" and chronic health problems. Once Louie did not want his older sister Judith to go out on a date. "As frail as Louie was," he recalled, "she pushed the piano in front of the door so that Judith could not get out."[13] This strong will was tempered with generosity and concern, however. One time, as Louie boarded the train for a Primary excursion, she, in a gesture of kindness, gave Bud a five-dollar gold piece as she departed—a notable sum for a young boy to receive. She involved him in the Primary Red Cross drive during World War I and in helping to get the *Children's Friend* mailed out after it came off the press.[14] Bud later gave one of his sons the middle name of Bouton out of respect for Louie.

Later in her life, Louie shared her feelings with her Primary associates: "Perhaps, like me, there are some who have been denied the great privilege of being a mother. . . . But God has given me many, many lovely children through other mothers, that I may pray for, think of, and love as I love you, my sisters. I feel that you are all my children, and your children, my grandchildren, or great-grandchildren."[15]

"A Most Wonderful Influence" over Children

In 1871, Louie began attending the Eleventh Ward Retrenchment Association meetings, which were held in the home of Mary Ann Freeze. When the Salt Lake Stake board for the Young Ladies Mutual Improvement Association (the new name for the Retrenchment Association) was organized in 1878, Mary Ann was called as president and Louie as her counselor. At the same time, Joseph Felt was called as the Salt Lake Stake YMMIA president and served in that capacity for eighteen years.

One month after Aurelia Spencer Rogers organized the first ward Primary in the Church and gathered together the children of Farmington, Utah (a community twenty miles north of Salt Lake City), for the Church's first Primary meeting, Eliza R. Snow chose Louie to be president of the Eleventh Ward Primary Association on September 14, 1878. As her counselors, Louie selected Elizabeth Mineer Felt, her sister-wife, and Louise Morris White.

The Eleventh Ward's first Primary meeting was held in the rock meetinghouse on First South and Eighth East in Salt Lake City. Eliza R. Snow, president of the Relief Society, and Eliza's counselor, Zina D. H. Young, attended this meeting, along with forty-three children. Interest in Primary grew and attendance soon averaged more than one hundred children each week. Under the direction of Eliza, Primary organizations were organized in several other wards in Salt Lake City and surrounding areas during the next few months. More followed, although at times some wards resisted organizing a Primary. Leaders in each ward provided their own lessons, music, and programs. According to May Anderson, who later served as second Primary general president, "If they needed heat, they must chop wood and carry coal if there was coal to be had."[16]

"Louie had a most wonderful influence over the little children of the Eleventh Ward," Lillie Freeze observed. "They were fascinated by her gracious manner. Every child was willing and anxious to do whatever she suggested."[17] According to the ward's Primary minutes, "The little children opened and closed the meetings with prayer, then they stood upon their feet and bore testimonies of the Lord's goodness to them and to others, and expressed the desire they had to do right."[18] The children visited and prayed for sick children; donated money to the building of the Salt Lake Temple; and accompanied Louie and her counselors on walks, outings to Liberty Park, and excursions to the Great Salt Lake. The Primary children's choir presented concerts to send a missionary to England and to bring a Latter-day Saint family to Utah. The *Deseret News* reported that children also participated in a Primary Fair, for which the children made "cardboard brackets, dressed dolls, wool flowers, mouse traps, doll cradles, picture frames, patchwork blocks, embroidered mottoes, hemstitched handkerchiefs, hair pin cases, jumping horses, baby shoes, embroidered collars, daisy mats, hair flowers, wax ornaments, scarfs, wool mats, plaster work, book shelves, moss mats, letter cases, wool baskets, cornucopias, boats, crochet tidys, match cases, etc. Pies and cakes made by the children and cabbages, corn, potatoes, beans, etc., which they had raised were also on exhibition."[19]

When Louie was released as ward Primary president, she and her counselors made a wreath from the hair of the Primary children—a popular keepsake in the nineteenth century. In addition, the women in the presidency dressed identically and had their picture taken together. They gave the wreath and photograph to Eliza R. Snow, thanking her for the opportunity to serve in the first Primary in Salt Lake City.

The First General Primary President

One day Aurelia Spencer Rogers, organizer and president of the first ward Primary, came from Farmington to visit her sister, Ellen Spencer Clawson, president of the Twelfth Ward Primary in Salt Lake City. Eliza R. Snow also visited the same Primary. There Eliza discussed with Aurelia the idea of having a general president over the Primary associations that had been organized in numerous wards. She asked Aurelia to suggest the name of a woman to serve as president, and when Aurelia suggested Louie B. Felt, Eliza said that was her choice as well.[20]

When Eliza approached Louie about serving as general president of the Primary, Louie hesitated because she felt unqualified and unprepared. But when Eliza told her it was a call from the priesthood, she replied, "I will do the best I can."[21]

In June 1880, the women of the Salt Lake Stake, which at the time included all of Salt Lake County, met together in the Tabernacle for a two-day conference. During the morning meeting on June 19, Church President John Taylor announced the calling of Louie B. Felt as Primary general president. In the same meeting, Eliza R. Snow was named the Relief Society general president and Elmina Shepard Taylor the YLMIA president. Louie chose Matilda M. Barratt and Clara C. M. Cannon as counselors, Lillie T. Freeze as secretary, and Minnie Felt as treasurer. She was set apart by President Taylor. (When Matilda Barratt was released as first counselor in 1888, Lillie Freeze became counselor; she served until 1905, followed by May Anderson. Josephine R. West followed Clara Cannon as second counselor in 1895 and served until 1905. Clara W. Beebe then served in that position.) The first stake Primary board, in the Salt Lake Stake, was also organized that day.

Referring to Louie, Lillie wrote, "Her charming magnetic personality her sweet winning ways her peculiar . . . adaptability in handling children made her the idol of the day—she was sought after by women and children, feted, praised, and honored and adored." She added that "no woman in the Church has been more beloved no woman has received such manifestations of loving admiration from co-workers especially from her own board no woman filled the position better no one is entitled to more honor."[22]

Although she did not want to be in the limelight, Louie dedicated her life to carrying out the work to which she had been called. She thus sought counsel from others whom she considered more experienced leaders. According to Lillie, she "was in constant counsel with E. R. Snow, Aurelia S. Rogers, E. B. Wells, Zina D. Young and other prominent sisters."[23]

During the first decade of her administration, Louie was more involved with her ward Primary than with general administrative matters, and the work of Primary was centered on the ward and stake levels. Until 1885, she held three offices at once: ward Primary president, stake YLMIA counselor, and general Primary president. Therefore, when she attended conferences she spoke as a YLMIA representative more often than as a Primary one.

For the Jubilee celebration (the fiftieth anniversary) of the Church in 1880, the Primary organizations in Salt Lake created a float for the Pioneer Day parade on July 24. The officers decorated Brigham Young's sleigh, the *Julia Dean,* had it mounted on wheels, and arranged for it to be pulled by white horses. Forty-two children, a boy and girl from each of the twenty-one wards in the city, sat in the sleigh. Louie Morris White wrote, "Some days before the Twenty-fourth, Sister Felt came to me and said, 'I have come to see if you will ride with the children in the parade. That is where I would like to be, but they tell me I must ride in a carriage with my two counselors in the General Board and represent that organization."[24]

In 1883, Louie and Joseph traveled to Morgan, a town northeast of the Salt Lake Valley, where they boarded the train and rode back to Salt Lake City with Louie's mother, Mary Bouton, and her brothers, Homer and Frank, and sister, Lillie, who were coming from Joseph Bouton's funeral in Connecticut. On board the train also was May Anderson, a young convert who had emigrated with her family from Liverpool, England. Once she was settled in the valley, May and her mother visited the Felt home in Salt Lake City. Though Louie was fourteen years older than May, they became close friends. Once when Joseph Felt had to go on a business trip, he asked May to stay with Louie, who was ill. She ended up staying for nearly thirty years as a friend, companion, helper, and later as a Primary counselor to Louie.

Louie conducted the first Primary general conference, held October 5, 1889, in the Assembly Hall. The conference was attended by twenty-five women from Cache, Box Elder, Salt Lake, Utah, Juab, Sanpete, Sevier, and St. George stakes. She stated that the purpose of the conference was "to encourage, counsel and advise for the mutual benefit and advancement of the Primary associations."[25]

Inasmuch as the general Primary did not have any operating funds, Joseph Felt paid for his wife's expenses, railroad tickets, and books. He also paid for May to accompany Louie on many visits to stakes throughout the Utah Territory. Occasionally, stakes paid the visitors' expenses.

Travel was often difficult for Louie, who was at times partially paralyzed. Most of the time she did not have good health, in fact. Once her foot was so swollen with rheumatism that she could not wear a shoe. Undaunted, she wore a shoe on one foot and a slipper on the swollen one and continued her work.

The Kindergarten Movement

President Wilford Woodruff issued the Manifesto in 1890, which ended polygamy and paved the way for Utah to gain statehood in 1896. When the territorial legislature passed the Free Public School Act the same year establishing tax-supported public schools, church and state were thus separated educationally. At the Primary conference in October 1890, Louie counseled, "If there was a time when it was important to attend to the spiritual education of our children, it is now when so many of our little ones attend the district schools, where religion is forbidden to be taught. . . . [It is] necessary to take a more general interest in the welfare of the souls of our little children."[26] At that time, however, Primary was not seen as the vehicle for accomplishing this and religion classes were established instead by the leaders of the Church. Children in elementary school attended religion class, usually on Thursdays, for religious instruction. As a result, two organizations had responsibility for children: religion classes, under the direction of the priesthood, and Primary, under the direction of women, who at the time did not have a line of authority or network of communication with the General Authorities. In fact, it was not until 1907 that priesthood advisers, Elders Hyrum M. Smith and George F. Richards, were appointed to the Primary—the first auxiliary to have such. The first general board was comprised of five members only—three members of the presidency, the secretary, and the treasurer. Five more members were added in 1892 and two more in 1893, including Aurelia Spencer Rogers. When Louie was released some thirty years later, there were twenty-five board members and two honorary members.

Louie expected board members to be punctual in attending board meetings and to stay for the entire meeting, dress appropriately, show reverence, and support the Brethren.[27] She led the Primary with love and interest in each person with whom she worked.

During a visit to one stake, Louie received a note asking her to come to the home of a sick child. When she and her companions arrived at the home, they could see that the child was critically ill. The anxious mother asked Louie to pray for her son. According to May Anderson, Louie, who had the "gift of prayer," knelt beside the boy and an offered an earnest plea for the child to live. Months later, she received a letter from the grateful mother and a picture of her healthy son. Years later, this boy visited Louie as he departed on his mission.[28]

May Anderson wrote about another excursion: "One very hot day a white top [buggy] with two members of the General Board and three stake officers started at day break to meet with the Primary Association of one of the small wards in the Snake River country. The Primary officers of the ward had been notified by letter that we would be there about 10:00 A.M. Our stake president was the driver and she knew how to handle horses so this time we were not so very nervous. We had been going about an hour when we reached a bridge which crossed the Snake River where it was deep and wide, but the bridge had gone and we couldn't drive across. At that time there were few homes or even towns in that section and no such convenience as a telephone. There was only one thing to do, turn back to the nearest cross roads and find another way to reach and keep our assignment. We finally arrived there, two hours late. The little meeting house built of lumber stood in the blazing sun, not a tree in sight to suggest shade. As we came closer we decided that surely we were too late. But, no, around the building were grouped a few big heavy wagons indicating how the congregation had traveled and that they were still there.

"When we entered the room it was packed with women and children, the floor was bare, a little table at one end served for the pulpit, on it was a bunch of wild flowers, somewhat wilted with the heat. A path was made for us to reach the table, but to get there it was necessary to step carefully, for on quilts spread under and around the table were babies and little children, most of them asleep.

"But one can never forget how we were received. The mothers picked up their babies and all stood and sang for us the song of welcome that had been prepared in our honor."[29]

Camilla C. Cobb, daughter of Karl G. Maeser, the founder of Brigham Young Academy, opened the first kindergarten in Utah in 1874. Later, she helped organize the Utah Kindergarten Association in 1895, with the assistance of Relief Society, YLMIA, and community leaders, including Sarah M. Kimball, Isabella Horne, Elmina S. Taylor, Zina D. H. Young, Bathsheba W. Smith, and Ellis R. Shipp. Church President Wilford Woodruff endorsed the new organization. Since Camilla served in the Primary presidency of the Salt Lake Stake, she knew both Louie Felt and May Anderson and probably introduced the kindergarten concept to them. In 1895, May and Louie attended a kindergarten training class taught by a graduate of the Boston Training School, Alice Chapin, who had come to Salt Lake City.

Early Primary classes followed the same pattern as education in the United States in the latter part of the nineteenth century, where children learned by drill and by rote. Primary children often recited questions and answers and catechisms written by Eliza R. Snow. The educational movement in the 1890s became developmental and child-centered, focusing on the child's nature and needs and viewing the teacher as a leader rather than a taskmaster. Learning was accomplished through activity, art, play, experimentation, freedom, curiosity, and interest. (Writings of national leaders of progressive education, including Francis Parker, John Dewey, and G. Stanley Hall, would later be published in the *Children's Friend*.)[30]

After receiving their diplomas from the training class, Louie and May opened a private kindergarten in the basement of the Eleventh Ward meetinghouse. Louie, who taught for two years, also served on the board of the Mormon Utah Kindergarten Association. (Several other churches and community groups had formed their own kindergarten associations; for example, the Free Kindergarten Association was organized by women of other faiths and the Women's Christian

Temperance Union.) In 1896, various kindergarten associations, such as the Salt Lake Kindergarten Association, the Free Kindergarten Association, and the Utah Kindergarten Association, merged into the Utah State Kindergarten-Primary Association.

Louie and May's kindergarten training and teaching had a profound influence on the development of Primary. Lillie observed: "From that time the Primary began to take on definite and steady growth."[31] The two women saw ways to implement child-centered education into Primary. Following the trend of Utah schools of dividing children into age groups, they instituted graded classes in their ward Primary. They found that lessons geared to the various levels of children's development eliminated many discipline problems and improved attendance. Discipline problems had been a major complaint of Primary leaders, who often had to manage a hundred children in one room. With ample evidence of the Eleventh Ward's success, Louie, as general Primary president, suggested that local associations divide children's classes into three different age groups. The second outgrowth of Louie and May's participation in the kindergarten movement was their instituting mothers' classes in Primary to teach mothers how children learn.

Since a general curriculum had not yet been developed, local leaders were responsible for developing their own Primary lessons. At the 1896 Primary conference, the general leaders provided an outline for Primary work. They also printed a booklet the following year with suggestions for celebrating the 1897 Jubilee year, the fifty-year anniversary of the Saints entering the Salt Lake Valley.

Under Louie's direction, the general board celebrated the Jubilee event by publishing *Life Sketches of Orson Spencer and Others, and History of Primary Work* by Aurelia Spencer Rogers. To pay for its publication, the general officers asked each ward to donate money, the first board request for funds to support a churchwide project. They honored Aurelia at a surprise party on her sixty-third birthday in the Fourteenth

Ward Assembly Hall at which the book's publication was announced.

Money for operating local Primary organizations had been generated by annual ward celebrations. Then, in 1898, the general board requested that such monies be divided in thirds for the ward, stake, and general boards, thus providing the general board with operating capital. In 1899, the general board published the *Book of Instructions,* which explained how Primary groups should be graded.

Publishing the Children's Friend

At the beginning of the new century, Louie wrote in the *Woman's Exponent:* "So many changes have come to pass in our actions toward children and in our methods in rearing and training, that much might be said or written about them.

"We have much to be grateful for to Pestalozzi and Froebel and many others who have filled our own and our children's lives with pleasures and experiences of object lessons, and the Kindergarten, with its many beautiful phases, none of which appeal more strongly than the pleasures of 'learning by doing.'

"And as the care of children is woman's special charge, the new century will see much advancement and many things which today are in the experimental stage will be proven and tested, and whatever is unworthy will be cast out."[32]

The Primary general presidency, seeing a great need to communicate regularly with the stakes and wards, approached the First Presidency several times for permission to publish a journal but were told each time that it was too costly. In 1899, to provide some assistance for teachers, Louie requested William A. Morton, a writer of children's books, to publish a periodical called the *Primary Helper.* A collection of poems, songs, recitations, and scriptural stories, it lasted only a few issues and did not accomplish the widespread communication the Primary needed. Finally, in 1901, President Joseph F. Smith gave approval for a publication, on the condition that the Primary manage it themselves and keep out of debt. Louie offered her own home as collateral, and May resigned from her teaching position at the University of Utah in order to work on the new magazine.

When the general board met on November 18, 1901, they named the magazine the *Primary Friend*. Olive D. Christensen, a board member, prepared material to advertise the new magazine and inadvertently called it the *Children's Friend*. Feeling the misnomer a better choice, the board approved the change. The first issue was well received, and by the end of the year, the magazine paid for itself. The *Children's Friend* was initially a magazine to assist leaders and teachers, with lesson helps for the three grades and instructions for leaders, but it did not have any illustrations or materials for children.

Annual meetings for Primary workers provided another means of communication. Only stake Primary presidents attended the first general Primary meeting, held in 1889. Several years later, however, the general presidency decided that such conferences should include all stake and ward leaders. Accordingly, the first Primary general conference was held May 29, 1902. By 1904, the Primary moved its conference to coincide with the YLMIA and YMMIA June conference.

To house the magazine and the general board, the Primary rented a small room in the Templeton Building in downtown Salt Lake City. By 1909, the Bishops' Building, located on the east side of Main Street across from Temple Square, was completed, and the Primary, along with the Relief Society and YLMIA, moved to the new building.

In 1902, the Primary instituted a nickel fund, to which children and leaders were asked to contribute a nickel annually, to finance the general board's expenses and to replace previous methods of funding. This income covered transportation costs and office expenditures but not the publication costs of the *Children's Friend*.

Under Louie's guidance, the Primary continued to incorporate methods of the new or progressive education, with an emphasis on storytelling, thought questions, and activities such as singing, dancing, drama, arts and crafts, and handiwork. They further refined the curriculum by creating five age groups with two levels within each group: Group I included four- and five-year-olds; Group II, six- and seven-year-olds; Group III, eight- and nine-year-olds; Group IV, ten-and eleven-year-olds; and Group V, twelve- and thirteen-year-olds.

Each month ward Primary organizations carried out a designated theme in the four weekly meetings: Lesson Hour; Busy Hour, with crafts and homemaking and gardening projects; Story Hour; and Social Hour, with games and dances.[33] The Primary children met together for opening exercises each week and then separated for classwork. The Primary sought to provide midweek religious instruction, encourage recreational activities, promote good health habits, and prepare boys to receive the priesthood.[34]

The Primary Children's Hospital

Although the First Presidency granted approval for a children's unit at the Groves LDS Hospital in 1911, it did not actually open until 1913 when a new addition to the hospital was built to accommodate it. Two hospital rooms—one for boys and one for girls—comprised the children's unit, which was partially funded by voluntary donations from Primary children. Over the next few years, this limited space became inadequate to handle the number of children who needed medical care.

As a result, Louie and May visited convalescent hospitals in the East in 1921 to learn of modern practices, but they were disappointed at how little new information they gained. They felt that they were pioneering in this field and would need to devise their own program. The Church, under the direction of Presiding Bishop Charles W. Nibley, offered and renovated the large Hyde home on North Temple, north of Temple Square, for a new hospital, which was called the LDS Children's Convalescent Home and Day Nursery. Dedicated by President Heber J. Grant, it officially opened May 11, 1922. While the Church donated the building and equipment and cared for the grounds, the Primary was responsible for the care and expenses of patients and for administrative matters. Surgery was still performed at LDS Hospital, but children recuperated at the convalescent home.

May Anderson said of this convalescent home, the first of its kind in the Intermountain West: "When this idea was first presented, there was in all this intermountain country no place for special care of afflicted and crippled children. Surely the thought came because there was a real need for this type of service."[35] During the hospital's thirty years of operation, nearly six thousand children received inpatient treatment and nearly four thousand received outpatient care.

To keep pace with the increasing number of children being treated and the advancements in medical technology, more funds were needed. General board member Nelle Talmage suggested asking members of the Church to annually donate a penny for each year of their age. This program, which came to be called the Penny Parade, provided almost enough money to finance the hospital and also helped accomplish one of Louie's goals by providing opportunities for Primary children to give service to others.

Following the child-centered and activity-oriented concepts of the new education, the revised Primary curriculum in 1912 also included social activity, ethics, and music. In 1913, the Primary held its first training seminar for Primary teachers, which lasted six weeks. The general leaders invited each stake to send one representative, for whom the general board paid transportation costs. Each delegate would then return home to teach the stake board, who would in turn teach the ward leaders. One hundred and twenty-six women attended the first seminar and received instructions in lesson development, story telling, music, physical education, domestic science, and handiwork.

Church leaders became concerned when they saw that as always, children had too much leisure time and needed more formal teaching. Thus, the Primary and the YLMIA and YMMIA focused on social and ethical training and activities while Sunday School, religion classes, and priesthood quorums taught Church history and doctrine and the scriptures.

During World War I, many Primary children planted war

gardens and assembled Red Cross supplies. The general presidency, who suggested a large-scale effort by individual Primary organizations to make articles for soldiers, set up a display of samples at the 1917 October general conference. Primary children made more than one hundred thousand articles, including such items as washcloths, tray covers, bed socks, afghans, shoulder wraps, and hot water bag covers.[36] During the devastating flu epidemic of 1918–19, in an attempt to halt spread of the disease, Louie directed local Primary leaders not to hold meetings.

It was during this period of her administration that Louie received unexpected honors. Her co-workers planned a party to celebrate her sixty-first birthday, May 5, 1911. Five years later, at the 1916 Primary conference, the Salt Lake Stake presented a festival in her honor in which more than fifteen hundred Primary children sang and danced.[37]

Louie's Release and Last Years

From its inception, Primary had been responsible for children to age fourteen. But with twelve-year-old boys receiving the Aaronic Priesthood and the Church's adoption in 1913 of the Boy Scout program, which included boys twelve to eighteen years of age, the First Presidency transferred twelve- and thirteen-year-old boys from Primary to the YMMIA. In 1925, the Primary introduced a new program for ten- and eleven-year-old boys called the Trail Builders. Twelve- and thirteen-year-old girls, however, remained in Primary, but during the 1920s they enjoyed a more vigorous program than before. They participated in planning for and teaching both their own and younger age groups.

By age 75, Louie was in poor health, and she asked for a release, which was extended on October 6, 1925, at general conference. During her forty-five years as president, though childless, she "mothered" one hundred thousand children and guided and supervised thirty thousand officers.[38] She was made an honorary general board member following her release.

A general board member wrote in tribute to Louie: "Not

only has she intelligently directed the affairs of the Primary Association of the church but she has held the sisters together in love. The General Board has been devoted to her and ever willing to do whatever she has asked of them. Her heart has been full to overflowing with sympathy, she has always understood conditions in our homes, her heart has gone out to the husbands and the little ones. When we have had trials and worries which have almost overwhelmed us, we have taken them to her and she has blessed us by the Spirit of God, and given us faith and courage and strength to bear our burdens. When we have left our families and gone out into the stakes to carry the Primary messages, she has inquired daily about conditions in our homes and has anxiously awaited our return."[39]

During Louie's last years, her failing health was a difficult challenge for her. In addition, May Anderson had moved out a few years before Louie's release. For more than forty years May had been a part of the Felt household. Their lifelong friendship remained a treasured memory spanning the many years of Louie's marriage as well as the lonely years of her early widowhood after Joseph's death in 1907. After May left, Louie lived alone in an apartment and had only occasional visitors. A friend remarked that her "smile has not been as bright as it used to be, and her words are not quite so cheerful."[40] One issue of the *Children's Friend* suggested that Primary classes pay her a visit. Louie died February 13, 1928, at home at the age of seventy-seven.

Louie's tenure as general president still stands as the longest of any auxiliary president in the history of the Church. She helped shape Primary in significant and enduring ways during her lengthy administration. Although programs have changed to some degree with passing years, two of the projects she instituted, the *Children's Friend* and the Primary Children's Hospital, have influenced and blessed the lives of thousands of children for almost a century. Though Louie Bouton Felt never gave birth to children, she raised children and grandchildren of a sister-wife, devoted her life to children, and was indeed the children's friend.

2

May Anderson

1925–1939

*M*ay Anderson showed an interest in writing early in her life in Liverpool, England. As a new convert to The Church of Jesus Christ of Latter-day Saints, she wrote several stories that were read in Church meetings. Others recognized her talents and their potential for good. One missionary, impressed by her ability, promised her that if she developed her talent for writing, she would eventually write for the children of the Church.[1] Another missionary, who stopped at the Anderson home one day to visit, placed his hand on May's shoulder and said to her mother, "Sister Anderson, the time will come when the name of this little girl will be known all over Zion."[2] Not only did May Anderson write for the children of the Church and serve as the first editor of the *Children's Friend,* she also served as a counselor and then as general president of the Primary Association, and her name was indeed known "all over Zion." But even more significant than the prominence she achieved was her beneficial influence on the lives of the children she loved and served throughout her life.

From Scotland to Zion

May Anderson's mother, Mary Bruce, was born in 1837 in Burravoe, Scotland, and traced her lineage from Robert the Bruce, a fourteenth-century Scottish king who fought for his country's independence from England. May's father, Scott Anderson, was born in 1835 in Shetland, Scotland. Scott's work as a temperance lecturer took the young married couple to Liverpool, England.

Mary Jane Anderson (who acquired the name "May" as a young adult) was born June 8, 1864, in Liverpool, England, the fourth of twelve children. The Anderson children included twins Scott William (who died as an infant) and Robert, who were born in 1860. The next son was also named Scott William in memory of the twin who had died. Then Mary was born. Following Mary in birth order were Wilford, Harry, Nancy, Marian, Frederick, Helen, Catherine, and David. Because of Mr. Anderson's occupation, the family moved frequently. When Mary was eight years old, they moved to Ireland, living in the cities of Cork and Dublin. A few years later, the family returned to Liverpool.

As the eldest daughter in a large family, Mary was her mother's helper; but she also naturally loved children. She enjoyed teaching and playing with her younger brothers and sisters and was nicknamed "teacher."[3] She often shopped at the market for her mother and then rationed the food each day. According to an account in the *Children's Friend,* "Every child was given just so much butter on Monday and so much on Tuesday and she never allowed one of them to eat Tuesday's butter on Monday."[4] Mary made Christmas, birthdays, and holidays memorable for her younger brothers and sisters. She usually found time for herself only at night when all the children were in bed and she read by the fireplace—until her mother insisted she go to bed.

Once, Mary visited her Aunt Jane in Edinburgh, Scotland. When she returned, she regaled the other children with tales of sleeping in a four-poster bed and of Aunt Jane bringing her breakfast on a tray. Mary's wealthy grandmother lived in Liverpool and invited Mary to stay with her on several occasions. She remembered how her grandmother spent Saturdays in preparation for the Sabbath and insisted that Mary read the Bible with clean hands and a clean handkerchief.

Mary's father, an eloquent and witty speaker, traveled to

many cities to campaign against liquor. Occasionally, he would take Mary with him to recite "The lips that touch liquor shall never touch mine."

When the Andersons again lived in Liverpool, a family friend announced that he had joined The Church of Jesus Christ of Latter-day Saints. Mary's father told his friend that he was foolish for joining the Mormons. Nevertheless, the Anderson family began attending church out of curiosity. Three missionaries, Elders Orson Pratt, John Nicholson, and Charles W. Nibley, taught them the gospel. The two oldest boys, Robert and Scott W., asked to be baptized. Mr. Anderson, who did not drink liquor, was intrigued by some of the doctrines, particularly the Word of Wisdom. Yet he felt it would be unwise to join an unpopular sect, that doing so would hurt his business relations and standing in the community.

One day while working at home, he heard a voice call to him. When he asked his wife and children what was wanted, they replied that they had not called him. Three times he heard a voice telling him, "Scott Anderson, you must go to Zion." Moved by this manifestation, he went right to the missionaries and said he was ready to be baptized. Scott, his wife, and several of the children were baptized August 12, 1879. Mary was baptized by Elder John Nicholson and confirmed by Elder Orson Pratt.

Mary attended the branch in Liverpool with her family and participated in music, drama, and recitations. The elders asked her to write stories to be read in Church meetings, and she prayerfully did so.

The Andersons felt they must go to Zion but could not afford to all go at once. Therefore, Scott and two boys, Wilford (who was known as Will) and Robert, immigrated first. Mary, anxious to help with family finances, wanted to go with them to America to work, but when her mother objected, she obediently ended her trip preparations and stayed home. Robert went on to Utah, while Scott and Will remained in New York to work and to wait for Mrs. Anderson and other family members. Three children, Catherine, Harry, and Scott W., remained in England. Mary, her mother, and the rest of the family sailed with 427 other Saints and fourteen missionaries on the ship *Nevada,* arriving in New York on May 29, 1883.

The train on which they traveled west wrecked in Wyoming. The cars containing furniture were overturned, but none of the cars containing Church members or their luggage suffered any significant damage. The group of Saints held a prayer meeting to thank the Lord for protecting them. Train crews repaired the damage, and after only one day's delay, the Andersons and the other passengers continued on to Utah.

During this journey, five-year-old Nellie (Helen) caught a cold, which then turned into pneumonia. Mary was especially attentive to her fretful, sick little sister, even giving Nellie her prized necklace to play with. On this train trip nineteen-year-old Mary met thirty-three-year-old Louie Bouton Felt, who had boarded the train in Morgan, Utah (see chapter 1, page 13).

When the Andersons finally arrived in Salt Lake City, Robert greeted them and took them to a home he had rented. Having stocked the pantry with food, he had a fire burning in the stove and dinner ready for them to eat.

Nellie's pneumonia grew worse, and she died shortly after the family's arrival in Utah. The baby, David, also became seriously ill and died. Mary's mother was grief stricken. Trying to comfort and cheer her mother, Mary suggested they visit Joseph and Louie Felt, whom they had met on the train.

Louie and Mary became very close and lifelong friends. Primary associates later referred to them as "David and Jonathan" because of their friendship—they loved each other and the Primary work in which they were both engaged. Since Mary's mother, Louie's own mother, and another good friend, Mary Ann Freeze, were named Mary, Louie suggested to Mary Anderson that she change her name to May to avoid confusion. Although she had a strong personality, Mary adored Louie so much that she was willing to follow her wish. For the rest of her life, she was known by the name of May.

A Gifted Teacher

May found a job as a clerk at the R. K. Thomas and Company dry goods store but soon realized this was not satisfying to her. When Joseph Felt needed to take a six-week business trip, he invited May to stay with Louie, who was not well. May not only stayed six weeks to help Louie, but she also quit her job at the store and became a permanent member of the Felt household.

May, who had an unusual ability to work with children, wanted to be a teacher. An opportunity arose opening that door for her when, in 1895, May and Louie enrolled in a two-year kindergarten training course. May taught kindergarten for four years in a school she and Louie opened themselves. She was then asked to be an instructor at the University Training School at the University of Utah. The head of the department, Mary C. May, observed May's wonderful teaching ability and suggested that she pursue graduate studies at Columbia University in New York City. Although pleased by the confidence her supervisor placed in her, May did not pursue graduate school for she felt her life's path would take her in a different direction.

For five years, May served as a counselor to Louie in the Eleventh Ward Primary presidency. Living in Louie's home, she was a part of the family that consisted of Louie, Joseph, and his two other wives and their children. One of the Felt children said, "We all love Aunt May. We feel like we can tie to her, and she is always fair with us. 'Be fair' was and is one of her big lessons to us as children."[5] Another of the girls to whom she was "Aunt May" said, "We like her because she helps us be good."[6] Vera Felt, one of Joseph's daughters, was especially close to May.

Although May seems to have fit in well, becoming much like a family member, she was very strict and abrupt in manner and did not allow exceptions to household rules. Once when Bud Keysor, Joseph's grandson, missed his nine o'clock curfew by a few minutes, he found that May had locked the door and refused to let him in.[7]

May's Work in the Primary

May's calling to serve in the Primary at the general level was an outgrowth of her friendship with Louie B. Felt, who was appointed the general president in 1880. At the first annual Primary meeting in October 1889, although May was not a member of the general board or presidency, Louie requested that she take notes. A short time later, while the two women took a train trip to visit Primary units in Springville, Utah, Louie decided to call May, who often traveled as her companion, as an official Primary worker. May was somewhat reticent to accept the call because of her shyness and because she was afraid that she might have to pray in public. She also felt she didn't know enough about Primary work. Louie encouraged her to accept and then taught her a lesson about the Word of Wisdom. Having grown up in England, May loved to drink tea and found that when she tried to quit she got severe headaches. When Louie told her that she did not like to order a cup of tea for her, May promised to give it up. She never went back to her tea-drinking habit again.

May was officially sustained as the general secretary of the Primary Association on October 5, 1890. Fifteen years later, in 1905, she became first counselor to Louie. That year, she also supervised the publication of the *Primary Songbook.*

After Louie's husband, Joseph Felt, died in 1907, May continued to live in Louie's home. The two women became even closer as they served together in the Primary presidency and in that capacity launched two significant and enduring Primary projects: the *Children's Friend* magazine and a convalescent home that would later be known as Primary Children's Hospital.

May served a one-year appointment on the Children's Bureau of the U.S. Department of Labor during World War I. She was also a member of the Salt Lake Committee of Child Welfare.

The Children's Friend

Many local Primary leaders and teachers asked the general leaders for help in lesson preparation and for effective teaching methods. The general Primary leaders, in addressing this need, petitioned the First Presidency for a journal for their organization. Although their request was denied several times, President Joseph F. Smith granted approval for its publication on October 30, 1901, on the condition that the Primary leaders manage the magazine and provide their own financing. May was appointed editor at a salary of thirty dollars a month and served in that capacity for the next thirty-eight years.

As they labored on the first issue, Louie and May were excited about producing the *Children's Friend*. However, their printer shocked them when he told them, "Don't do it. Don't do it. Magazines run by women always fail. Take my advice and drop the idea."[8] Unable to respond, the women returned to their office. By the next day, with their spirits revived, they went back to the print shop and spoke to another man, who likewise tried to discourage them. Nevertheless, they examined paper samples, looked at type styles, and forged ahead.

The first issue of the *Children's Friend* appeared in January 1902 with a printing of 2,000 and contained lessons for three grades, a greeting from the general Primary presidency, suggestions for teachers, and a poem, "Our Work and Our Wealth," by Lula Greene Richards, the first editor of the *Woman's Exponent*. Although initially the goal of the *Children's Friend* was to provide lesson ideas for leaders and teachers, later the magazine became more child-oriented, with color illustrations, stories, and articles for children.

During the early days of publication, Louie and May saved string and wrapping paper, hand-addressed the issues, and carried bundles of magazines from the Primary offices to the post office. Although sales were slow at first, by the end of the first year of publication, the magazine not only broke even but also made a small profit.

Years later, when W. W. Riter, the Church auditor, examined the financial records of the magazine, he asked where the

Primary had obtained the capital to start the publication. May replied, "We had none." He then asked, "What did you have to offer as collateral?" "We had nothing, Brother Riter," May said. "Our only assets were faith and a willingness to work."[9]

As a surprise to May, Louie included May's picture in the January 1912 issue of the *Children's Friend* so that readers could get acquainted with its editor. Louie wrote of May, "Although small in stature, she has wonderful force of character, resourcefulness, and business ability. But her greatest interest in life is the children. Nothing is too great a task if it will in any way be of benefit to them; their mental and physical welfare is her first thought."[10]

Although boys entered YMMIA at age twelve, girls stayed in Primary until age fourteen. In 1922, the Primary, at May's suggestion, introduced the Seagull program for the twelve- and thirteen-year old girls. She outlined as the purpose of the program preparing girls for YWMIA by giving them opportunities for developing leadership abilities and offering service. The Seagull girls, guided by an adviser, planned their own activities and filled requirements in five areas: spirituality, knowledge, service, health, and handicrafts.

Second General President

Early in her life, May received a patriarchal blessing from Church Patriarch Hyrum G. Smith in which she was told of her mission in life: "The Lord has been mindful of thee for good ever since thy birth; He has called thee out of the world in order to accomplish the mission which was given thee at an early period in thy life. He has also spared thy life to live and enjoy the blessings of that mission and ministry. And it is thy privilege to live and fulfill that mission in honor."[11]

When Louie B. Felt was released as Primary general president on October 6, 1925, May was sustained to succeed her. The change in presidency marked a significant change in their lives.

May's new calling, "her mission," fulfilled the promise given to her years before in her patriarchal blessing. With no children of her own, she became "Primary Mother" to more than a hundred thousand children. She selected Sadie Grant Pack and Isabella Salmon Ross as her counselors. Sadie served until October 1929, at which time Isabella became first counselor. Edna Harker Thomas succeeded Isabella as second counselor, serving until December 1933. Edith Hunter Lambert then became second counselor.

While May had had the unusual opportunity of having been tutored for forty-two years by her predecessor, she brought her own talents to the presidency—a bright mind, executive ability, and a deep understanding of and love for children. Frances Grant Bennett, a general board member, wrote, "Her first thought was always for the welfare of the children of the Church. It bothered her not at all if her plan was inconvenient for the teachers or difficult for the parents. 'What is best for the children?' she would say."[12]

May's co-workers considered her always candid, but they also said she was sometimes tactless. When Frances Bennett was called to the board, she reluctantly accepted the assignment because she had loved her stake Primary calling and because of May's reputation as a "very dictatorial and unbending 'old maid.'" She described May as "a short woman, with almost white hair cut short and worn in very precise waves. She had piercing blue eyes and a resolute chin and mouth. I wasn't looking forward at all to working closely with her.

"This feeling was not relieved in any way when at our first meeting she said to me, 'I really didn't want you on my board. Your name has been suggested to me a number of times; in fact, I have said to myself more than once, 'If worst comes to worst, there is always Frances Bennett.'

"'Sister Anderson,' I blurted out, 'what a thing to say to me!'

"'Oh, don't misunderstand me, my dear,' she said. 'It is only because you are your father's daughter that I didn't want you. I don't like the idea that you might run to your father with tales every time anything goes wrong.'" President Heber J. Grant, president of the Church from 1918 to 1945, was Frances's father.

Nevertheless, Frances served on the general board for six years, and after she was released because of poor health, she commented, "She no longer offended me with her blunt remarks; in fact, I enjoyed her utter frankness. . . . I consider it one of the choicest experiences of my life to have been so closely associated with May Anderson."[13] They remained close friends, and at May's request, Frances spoke at her funeral in 1946.

During May's administration, Primary was usually held on Monday afternoon after school and focused on activities. Religion class, instituted when public schools began in Utah in 1890, was usually held Thursday afternoon and offered religious instruction. A conflict arose among some leaders over organization loyalty and purpose, especially since a number of them had callings in both organizations. When the two organizations were consolidated in 1930 as the Primary Religion Class Association,[14] spiritual instruction became a significant part of the Primary curriculum. The name was again simplified to Primary.

The Primary, under May's direction, outlined its purposes: "To give week-day religious instruction to the children of the Church; to supervise and direct their leisure time activities; to encourage proper health habits."[15] Lessons focused on gospel principles and character development while activities included "programs, entertainments, festivals, picnics, nature walks, kite tournaments, pet and hobby shows, the preparation of rhythmic ensemble and harmonica bands; the making of articles for bazaars, for the homes, the ward and for the Children's Hospital; the equipment of play grounds; the making of fly traps, clean up campaigns, et cetera."[16] During the early years of May's presidency, the Primary further refined class divisions. The younger classes were called Beginners (preschool age); Group 1 and Group 2 (six- and seven-year-olds); and Zion's Boys and Zion's Girls, known as the Zeebees and Zeegees (eight- and nine-year-olds). Primary leaders introduced the Trail Builder program for ten- and eleven-year-old boys in 1925; the following year, they organized the Bluebird class for girls of comparable ages. Several years later, the Trail Builder and Home Builder groups were again realigned, with the nine-, ten-, and eleven-year-olds enrolled as Blazers, Trekkers, and Guides, and the girls of the same ages as Larks, Bluebirds, and Seagulls. Because boys over twelve years of age graduated to YMMIA but the girls, by directive of the First Presidency, did not, a new program for the twelve-year-old girls, called the Mi-Kan-Wees, was included in Primary. Also known as the Pathfinders, this class was discontinued in 1934 when the twelve- and thirteen-year-old girls were assigned to the YWMIA.[17]

The Great Depression in the United States during the 1930s affected the Primary program in much the same way it affected other Church programs, and financial challenges made necessary a strict economy. The Primary, along with the other auxiliaries, was financially self-sustaining, and its income from the Nickel Fund, instituted in 1902, decreased during this period. Because many Church members experienced financial difficulties, subscriptions to the *Children's Friend* also dropped. As a result, the editors cut back the number of pages and use of color in the magazine and printed lessons in a separate bulletin rather than in the magazine. In spite of economic hardship, however, the twenty-four board members and the general presidency increased their visits to stakes, especially to those outside Utah.[18]

The Primary Children's Hospital

When May became Primary general president in 1925, the LDS Children's Convalescent Home and Day Nursery had been operating at the converted Hyde home on North Temple for three years. Financing the hospital was one of Primary's greatest challenges, and a plan unique to this hospital was developed gradually over a period of time. First, Primary children throughout the Church were asked to donate "birthday pennies," one for each year of age. Then as more money was needed, the annual Penny Parade (also called the Penny Drive and Penny Appeal) was initiated. Once a year Primary teachers and officers canvassed homes in their wards asking all family members to donate a penny for each birthday. Workers later suggested that people be "generously old," giving at least two pennies per year. The hospital received donations of many kinds: quilts made by Bluebird and Seagull girls, fresh fruits and vegetables, home-canned foodstuffs, and gifts for the patients as well as medical services and volunteer work.

May envisioned a bigger and more adequate facility and proposed to the First Presidency that land be purchased and plans drawn for a new hospital. President Heber J. Grant gave his hearty approval and did much to facilitate the building of the hospital. The Church purchased property a few blocks from LDS Hospital on a hill overlooking the city, at Twelfth Avenue and D Streets, and authorized preliminary architectural work. For President Grant's eighty-second birthday, business leaders of the community honored him with a dinner, giving him a chest filled with one thousand silver dollars. Ever the business-man, President Grant suggested the dollars be sold for $300 each to raise money for the new hospital. That very evening several dinner guests purchased silver dollars. Enthusiasm and support was keen, but progress on the new hospital slowed when President Grant suffered a stroke. Work was delayed indefinitely when World War II broke out. Although she had been instrumental in the creation of the first Primary-sponsored medical facility for children and had devoted much of her life to its development, May would not live to see her dream of a large, up-to-date hospital realized.

Jubilee and Other Occasions

May, who had been part of the Primary organization for most of its history, presided over the Primary's Jubilee, or fifti-eth anniversary celebration, held June 8–10, 1928, and it was indeed a grand celebration. Twelve thousand eager children marched in "The Parade of Primaries" in Salt Lake City beside gaily decorated floats representing the one hundred stakes of the Church. Hundreds of Primary children participated in a pageant, staged at the University of Utah stadium, complete with a Jubilee queen and fifty attendants. On Sunday morning,

June 10, the Primary presented a program in the Tabernacle, which had been decorated with flowers made by Primary children. Particularly poignant for May was the tribute given to her dear friend Louie B. Felt, who had died just four months earlier.[19]

Ten years later, in 1938, the Primary's sixtieth anniversary and May's thirteenth year as general president were observed quietly. An article in the July 1938 issue of the *Children's Friend* listed various commemorative activities of the Primary's leisure-time program. Some activities, planned in cooperation with the Church Beautification and Church Security programs, included cleaning Church grounds of weeds and trash; planting trees, flowers, and shrubs; and cleaning Church buildings. Other activities included making dishtowels and dust cloths; gathering seeds; building and painting cupboards; holding fund-raising parties, plays, and banquets; making posters to emphasize work; and building and sweeping sidewalks.[20]

Also in 1938, the Salt Lake Council of Women, a community group of prominent women, selected May as one of eight women for their Hall of Fame. They commended her for her leadership in the Primary, her work with the convalescent center and her planning of Primary Children's Hospital, and her efforts in publishing the *Children's Friend*. At a ceremony held in Salt Lake City, she received a gold medal in recognition for her accomplishments. That same year, at the Primary's sixtieth year celebration held in the Tabernacle, May's co-workers presented her with a bouquet of forty-eight roses, one for each of her forty-eight years of service to the Primary.

Nelle A. Talmage, a member of the Primary general board during May's tenure as president, wrote an essay on May Anderson, "an unforgettable character," for a university course she was taking in 1941. She wrote, "Although in her contacts with adults she was sometimes undiplomatic, with children her soft musical voice, her lack of self consciousness, and her genuine joy in their association drew them to her knee. . . .

"She was not the sweet young thing who had chosen to be a kindergarten teacher for a career, but an elderly woman—when I first met her—with iron gray hair, clear blue eyes helped with rimmed glasses, a courageous mouth with a suggestion of determined strong-mindedness. Yet with what boldness could she speak against a superficial treatment of underprivileged children!

"I have seen her—tiny in stature, dainty in bearing, 'her spirits a-tip-toe'—face a suave, oily-tongued politician, and persuade him to go her way. She was indeed 'a one-way person' when the road stretched out for children's rights."[21]

When May received a letter from a class of girls asking her for her testimony, she wrote, "One cannot see in a blossom all the forces of nature that combine under natural conditions to produce the color, form and fragrance of a beautiful flower. My testimony concerning the truth of the Gospel as restored by the Prophet Joseph Smith seems to have grown in my soul and has flourished ever since the representatives of the Lord first entered our home and succeeded in converting my parents; and so it is to me as a flower of great beauty and fragrance. Today my reason is convinced and my assurance has no doubts concerning the divine mission of our Church and its power to carry on to its ultimate victory."[22]

Although Primary units had been organized in New Zealand and Mexico in the 1880s, in Hawaii and Canada during the 1890s, and in England in 1916, Primary became more international during May's administration, expanding to Sweden, Germany, Holland, Denmark, Switzerland, Scotland, and South America. Home and neighborhood Primary organizations helped reach Latter-day Saint children and children of other faiths in mission areas. Yet Primary work in many mission areas was difficult because of the long distances many members had to travel and the lack of both experienced leaders and materials suited for various cultures. As a result, Primary organizations in areas distant from the center of the Church were not always effective or long-lasting. Beginning in 1930, the *Children's Friend* published mission lessons monthly, but translation of these was up to each mission, and the lessons largely reflected American culture and values.[23]

May's Release

For nearly five decades—fourteen years as president, thirty-eight years as editor of the *Children's Friend,* and a total of forty-nine years in various capacities on the general level—May had served the children of the Church. On November 18, 1939, President Heber J. Grant met with the Primary general presidency and board to announce the presidency's release. Seventy-five-year-old May spoke to the board about her experiences in Primary, testifying that the promises given to her earlier in her life had been fulfilled, that she had been able to write for the children of the Church, and that her name had been known in "every hamlet in Zion." She also requested that twenty thousand dollars from Primary funds be given for the building of a new hospital.

Following her release as Primary general president, she continued as president of the hospital board for another five years.[24] The April 1940 issue of the *Children's Friend* featured May's picture on the cover and several articles written in tribute to her.

Primary had been May's life. For most of her adult years, she had lived in Louie Felt's home and did not have a home of her own. A year before Louie's release, May went to live with two of her sisters, Catherine and Marion, in Salt Lake City.

After her release from Primary work, May served as an ordinance worker in the Salt Lake Temple for several years. Ill for the last year of her life and hospitalized for the last month, she died June 10, 1946, at the age of eighty-two. Her funeral was held at the University Ward chapel in Salt Lake City. President David O. McKay, then a member of the First Presidency, said in tribute, "I call her a mother though she has never been blessed with a child. Motherhood consists of caring, loving and rearing children. God bless her for that."[25]

3

May Green Hinckley

1940–1943

While serving in Chicago with her husband, who presided over the Northern States Mission, May Green Hinckley wrote a monthly newsletter to all the missionaries and staff, concluding her column with these phrases: "Let us love. Let us serve. Let us work together."[1] Such words not only typified the spirit she exhibited during her missionary service, but they were also the theme of her life. Although she experienced some difficult challenges—losing both her parents as a child, marrying late in life, becoming stepmother to thirteen children and Primary leader to thousands—she approached each situation with a keen desire to love, to serve, and to cheerfully work things out. Comments from her stepson, President Gordon B. Hinckley, not only describe her role in the mission field but also are appropriate for all the roles she played throughout her life: "She was a friend to the missionaries. She knew how to talk to them. She knew something of their problems, their disappointments, their discouragements, and their difficulties. She knew how to reach down and give them a hug and words of encouragement and lift them in a wonderful and remarkable way."[2] Such was also her influence on her family, friends, co-workers, and Primary children and associates.

British Beginnings

Named after her birth month, May Green was born on the first day of May 1881, in Brampton, Derbyshire, England, to William and Lucy Marsden Green. She was the eighth of ten children born to the Greens between 1863 and 1886.

May's mother, Lucy Marsden, was only sixteen when she married William Green, a potter ten years her senior. They married in Brampton, England—William's home town and not far from Walton, where Lucy had been born. The newlyweds settled in Brampton, where their seven daughters and three sons were all born. Two of their daughters died in childhood.

Little is known of May's childhood or of how her mother, Lucy, came to be baptized a member of The Church of Jesus Christ of Latter-day Saints on May 20, 1878. Perhaps the death of Lucy's baby daughter earlier that year caused her to search for answers to life's questions. Whatever the reason, from the moment of her conversion, Lucy remained firmly committed to the gospel, even though her husband did not share her beliefs. The older children, Elizabeth, Ann, Henry, and Ada, were baptized in England in 1879. The following year William was baptized, and then Florence, in 1882. In 1891, May, then nine years old, was baptized in Salt Lake City, Utah.

Several of May's older brothers and sisters, anxious to go to Zion, left England and traveled to Salt Lake City around the year 1887. In about 1889, Lucy gathered her three youngest children—May, eight; Albert, six; and Laura, three—and immigrated to Salt Lake City. She hoped that William, her husband, would follow, but he never joined his family in America and never joined the Church. May never saw her father again. He died at age sixty-six on April 11, 1902, in Brampton, England. Her brothers later served as proxies for their father and performed his temple ordinances in the Salt Lake Temple. The family was finally sealed together in 1930.

Tragically, May's mother died in 1891, just two years after arriving in America. Only forty-five years old at the time, she left three children under the age of ten, including May. These children went to live with an older sister in Salt Lake City. The following year, 1892, the youngest child, Laura, died at age six.

Serving a Mission

May grew up in the Salt Lake Fifth Ward in the Pioneer Stake, where she taught in the Sunday School and in the Young Ladies' Mutual Improvement Association (YLMIA). She wrote "Pioneer Stake Sunday School Board" on the inside cover of the set of scriptures that she used throughout her life, and she underlined many scriptures in the Pearl of Great Price. She also underlined part of the testimony of the Three Witnesses in the front of the Book of Mormon, which may have had special meaning to her because of her mother's conversion to the Church.

As a young woman, May received a patriarchal blessing in which she was told that she would marry and be a mother to many children. It would be many years, however, before this blessing would be fulfilled, and it would be fulfilled in an unusual way.[3]

May did not have to wait long to be of service. In 1907, when she was twenty-six years old, she received a call to serve a mission to the Central States Mission. Upon her return in 1909, she attended the Forest Dale Ward in the Granite Stake and was again called to serve in the YLMIA. Both opportunities helped her develop her natural tendencies to love people, work hard, and help others.

"It Was Easy to Love May"

May had not yet married and she needed to support herself, so she studied accounting and bookkeeping and developed her natural gift for organization. She began to work for the Salt Lake Clinic, a medical facility, in 1916. She was the first manager of the clinic's business office and held that position for eighteen years.

In 1920, May was called to serve as the YLMIA president in the Granite Stake, a large stake with twenty-one wards. One of her greatest accomplishments during the twelve years she served in this calling was the creation of the Gleaner program. This program for girls eighteen and older was so successful that it was eventually adopted by the YLMIA on the general level.

Life changed dramatically for May in 1931 when she began to date a handsome widower, Bryant S. Hinckley. The president of the Liberty Stake in Salt Lake City and principal of the LDS Business College as well as manager of the Deseret Gymnasium, Bryant had lost his first two wives through death. His first wife, Christine Johnson, had died suddenly of appendicitis in 1908, leaving a large family that included Stanford, Lucille, Grant, Grace, Carol, Venice, Virginia, Wendel, Waldo, and Christine. His second wife, Ada Bitner, died from cancer on November 9, 1930, leaving five additional Hinckley children: Gordon, Sherman, Ruth, Ramona, and Sylvia, who were all living at home with their father when May met him.

Daughters Carol and Ramona remember well the evening when their father invited May to a family dinner to introduce her to his family. The children surrounded a long table set up in the library of their home at 845 East 700 South in Salt Lake City. All the children were there. Prior to her arrival, Bryant told his family that he would like to marry May and had asked if that would that be all right with them. "If anybody had said no, I don't know what would have happened," said Ramona with a laugh. "But it was easy to love May. She became a mother to both me and my younger sister." May and the children discussed what they would like to call her. When she suggested "Aunt May," Ramona felt immediately that "a real sticky question" had been settled.[4]

Sixty-four-year-old Bryant Stringham Hinckley and fifty-year-old May Green were married on February 22, 1932, in the Salt Lake Temple, and May moved into the Hinckley home on Seventh South. At last, the promise in her patriarchal blessing had been realized, for with her marriage to Bryant, she became stepmother to many children—thirteen living children in all. Ruth, one of Bryant and Ada's daughters, wanted to do something special to welcome May when Bryant brought her home from their honeymoon. She took some cold tomato juice to

May's room and said, "This is for you, and welcome." May drank the whole glass. Years later, May finally admitted that she hated tomato juice but had diplomatically drunk it because Ruth had given it to her and she wanted to start off on the right foot.[5]

May wanted to become a part of this large family without pushing aside the memory of Bryant's first two wives, Christine and Ada. She devised a wonderful way to do this. Gathering family photographs from nooks and boxes around the house, May began creating a scrapbook filled with pictures of Bryant as a child and of the home where he was born. Then she arranged photographs of each of the thirteen children, beginning with Bryant's oldest child. For those who were married, she added photographs of their spouses and their children. She also asked each of the older children to write a letter to their father telling him how much they loved him. They did so, and May added these letters to the scrapbook.

When the thick scrapbook was finished, May inscribed a poem on the first page and drew roses around the border. The poem read:

> *Bryant dear,*
> *It mars not the passing of present hours*
> *The recollection of fragrant flowers*
> *So with the sentiment of companions dear*
> *Who may have gone but yet are near*
> *I too add my sentiment of you*
> *Expressing the love of the other two*
> *You're a sweetheart, a lover true,*
> *A kind and dutiful husband too*
> *From the bottom of our hearts we say,*
> *We love you—Christine, Ada, and May.*

She presented this scrapbook of love to Bryant on Christmas Day 1933.

At the time, Gordon was serving a mission in England. He wrote:

> This is the first time in my life that I have not been at home for Christmas. While sitting before a boarding

house fire and watching the flames go up the chimney, pictures pass by and other memories of other Christmas days. There is the morning when pajama-clad we hurried downstairs long before the rooster in the backyard was awake. Such excitement. Bulging socks, games, horns, a bright sweater, candy and nuts and flowers. . . . We ran back upstairs blowing harmonicas to show all those wonderful things to you and mother. You were tired out. But you played with us and kissed us before sending us back to bed till daylight. During the day you pulled us up and down the street on your new sled and we knew you were the biggest, strongest man in the world.[6]

The scrapbook was only one of the many ways May tried to become a part of the family. Ever desirous of maintaining family unity, she planned a family gathering each year on Bryant's birthday, including an elaborate program with tributes, games, and songs that she and other family members wrote. "May wasn't particularly musical," said Carol Hinckley Cannon, a daughter of Bryant and Christine, "but she loved music. She was very clever at writing."[7] Because she wasn't a composer, May would write new words to existing tunes.

"Aunt May was a happy, cheerful person," Carol said. "She worked out a pattern of the Hinckley coat-of-arms and made a beautiful hooked rug to put in front of the fireplace. She was always doing something with her hands."[8] Indeed, May's hands were seldom idle; she enjoyed crocheting and tatting lace on handkerchief edges, playing Chinese checkers, and writing.

But more important than the projects or events that May created for the family were the love and devotion she gave to individual members. Carol's older sister, Lucile Hinckley Laxman, said, "Aunt May Green loomed as an important part of my life with her great love and ability to bring family unanimity."[9] Ramona Hinckley Sullivan said, "Aunt May made a big difference in my life. She took care of Sylvia and me. We got constant special attention that my dad couldn't give each of us alone. She was definitely a mother to Sylvia and me.

Sylvia was taking a lot of math in high school. Aunt May was a wiz at math and could help her. With all due respect to my mother, brothers, and sisters, she was the dominant figure in my life growing up. She just saw to it that you had what you needed."[10]

Gordon, who left on his mission about a year after his father married May, recalled, "She took hold of that family. We were not little children, but she took hold of that family, not in any officious way. I don't know that it was easy for her to step into our family, but she did well. She got along well with all of us. We all appreciated her. We all respected her. We all loved her.

"I remember a time when I was terribly discouraged over something, and I was sort of brooding. We had a big library in our home with bookcases all around with over a thousand books. I was sitting there reading, but not reading, just sympathizing with myself. She came in, and in a quiet, very understanding way talked to me. I don't know what the adversity was, but it didn't look to be much of an adversity after she had finished talking with me.

"I served a mission for two years, and she was always encouraging. I felt I had a very strong backer at home in her as well as my father and my brothers and sisters."[11]

May, who was tall and stately, was reserved in nature yet friendly and cheerful. Intelligent and diligent, she was anxious to learn, whether it was mathematics or managing a home. Until she married and left her job at the Salt Lake Clinic, she had worked in an office most of her life and had become very skilled at her profession. As a newly married woman, she wanted to become a good cook, homemaker, wife, and mother. She set about doing so with the same intensity and energy with which she had excelled as a business manager.

"Aunt May really pitched in and learned how to do housekeeping," said Ramona. "Two of her sisters, who had families, came to our house several different days while we were at school to teach Aunt May. She was a very good learner. I don't ever remember her wearing a house dress; she always wore business clothes and comfortable laced shoes."[12]

May had a gift for interior decorating. "When she came into our home, she bought a gorgeous dining room set and other things," Ramona recalled. "She fixed up the house with beautiful, high-quality, up-to-date furnishings."[13] Having grown up in meager circumstances, she was careful in how she spent money and loved to shop for high-quality merchandise at bargain prices.

Cooking for a large family didn't come easily to May, who worked to learn this skill with the same tenacity and vigor with which she attacked any task. She bought two thick cookbooks with numerous menu suggestions. "She would lay them out on the kitchen table, and she would follow the recipes right down to the smallest detail," Ramona said. "She wore a big apron over her dress when she cooked, the kind you put your arms through. She also experimented with some special English cooking. When she found something that worked, she stuck with it. Therefore, she prepared the same menu for each Monday, another menu for each Tuesday, etc."[14]

The girls also remembered that May could recharge her energy unnoticed. "Aunt May was constantly busy, but she could take cat naps. She wore hats a lot so when she was on a bus or waiting, she'd just close her eyes and her hat would hide her face enough so that no one could tell she was napping. Her head wouldn't bobble or anything."[15]

Bryant said of their marriage: "Our married life was a happy one. . . . May was an extraordinary woman, with very little formal education. . . . She was a strong and expressive character, gifted as a leader, and could have distinguished herself as an actress. She understood poor people perfectly and won their confidence and following. She was methodical, original, resourceful, and a wonderful leader and a great and good woman."[16] Gordon felt that she helped make life smooth in their home. He said, "She thought before she spoke, and that's a tremendous virtue. She could pour oil on troubled waters. There are little differences that occur in every family, in the very nature of family life, and she knew how to subdue those feelings. And we're a strong-willed, outspoken family. I never heard her, in all my experience, give an unkind retort to any-thing that was said."[17]

May extended her concern beyond Bryant's immediate family. Bryant's father, Ira Nathaniel Hinckley, lived in Provo with his granddaughter Carol Hinckley Cannon. May wrote rhymes and limericks for him and remembered his birthday with a note or card. "The thing that I remember most about Aunt May," said Carol, "was that she was very mindful of other people. She wanted to cheer them up, especially those who were less fortunate."[18]

After a while, May missed her work at the Salt Lake Clinic and decided to return to work part-time. Someone else had been hired to replace her as the business manager so she did clerical work. She invited Ramona to work in the office with her. "She would have me lick the stamps and envelopes and made me feel like I was working in a business office," Ramona recalled.[19] May continued to work at the office until her hus-band was called to serve as a mission president.

The Northern States Mission

In 1935, Bryant S. Hinckley received a call to serve as president of the Northern States Mission. He and May, accom-panied by twenty-year-old Ramona and sixteen-year-old Sylvia, left for the mission headquarters in Chicago in January 1936. Ruth, Gordon, and Sherm, all young adults, remained at home in Salt Lake City.

Among the first things May did in the mission field was to brighten up the large, old mission home. She purchased yellow-striped fabric to replace the dark coverings on the fur-niture and painted the walls light colors to warm the interiors. "She loved to shop for a bargain and did much of the work herself," said Ramona. "She knew all about prices because she had worked with figures all her life."[20]

The newly freshened mission home provided a com-fortable place for visiting General Authorities to stay. Presi-dent Heber J. Grant visited often, as did his counselors, President J. Reuben Clark, Jr., and President David O. McKay.

The mission home was the residence of two sister missionaries as well as the Hinckleys. Next door lived several sets of elders who came to the home for their meals. Although May hired a cook to prepare the food, she made sure the missionaries and guests were served nutritious meals.

Not long after moving into the mission home, May, true to her organizational nature, made a large chart and attached it to a wall. Labeling slots in the chart with the various areas of the mission—Indiana, Illinois, Michigan, Ohio, Iowa, and Wisconsin—she placed on the chart the pictures and names of the missionaries according to where they were serving. When missionaries were transferred, she moved their pictures on the chart; when new ones arrived, she made sure their pictures were added; and when they left, the pictures came down.

About twice a month, May accompanied her husband on visits to the conferences held throughout the mission. Ramona and Sylvia often traveled with their parents to these conferences. Bryant recorded that they traveled 75,000 miles during the course of their mission. With no freeways, travel throughout the six-state area was often tedious and tiring. May met with the local auxiliary leaders, most of whom had never held leadership positions before, and gave them leadership support and training. She quickly recognized each leader's strengths and knew just how to help others serve to the best of their ability. And her great organizational ability always left each unit stronger.

Bryant praised May as his companion and assistant, writing that "May did a marvelous work as 'Mission Mother' and as President of the Relief Society of the Mission and the Young Ladies' organization. . . . [She] won the hearts of the people wherever she went. We made many dear friends in that mission."[21]

May was a friend to whom the missionaries could turn for comfort, encouragement, and medical help. Because her work at the Salt Lake Clinic had increased her knowledge of health care, she often knew what to do when one of the missionaries became ill. If not, she took the missionary to a doctor. In most areas of the mission, there were Latter-day Saint doctors or medical students willing to help without charge.

During the time the Hinckleys served in the Northern States Mission, the first stake in Chicago was created by President Heber J. Grant, which according to Bryant, brought the Church "a lot of publicity."[22] The Carthage Jail was also restored. To celebrate the restoration, the Church held a commemoration on June 27, the anniversary of the day on which the Prophet Joseph was martyred. Approximately seven hundred people attended, including President George Albert Smith of the Quorum of the Twelve, many missionaries, and other Church members. After a ceremony in Carthage and then in Nauvoo, commemorating the centennial of the founding of that city, May arranged tours of historic homes and sites. Bryant noted that the number of visitors was almost equal to the population of Nauvoo and that the townspeople were most hospitable in providing lodging and food.

Bryant was a great fan of Abraham Lincoln. Just a month after the Hinckleys arrived in Chicago, they planned to attend a Lincoln Day program at the opera house. Although May and Bryant had their tickets in hand, the show was so popular that when they arrived at the performance, they were informed that their seats had been given away an hour before. Disappointed, Bryant was ready to leave, but May walked over to a doorman and said, "We are from Salt Lake City. We would like to see this program. We have our tickets, but cannot get in. Can you help us? If you would come to Salt Lake City, we would show you a pleasant time." With that, the doorman escorted them to two of the best seats in the house.[23]

May's talents were wide-ranging. At a Church program in Chicago's Logan Square, with a number of professional musicians from the area performing, May, who had been trained in elocution, dressed in costume and read a piece she had written entitled "When Bryant Took Up Tomato Juice." Her husband noted, "She stole the show completely. It was a surprise to everybody."[24]

Although May occasionally "stole the show," her main goal was in helping others achieve and in bringing out the best in those with whom she associated. Ramona was talented in art, and while the family lived in Chicago, May enrolled her in the Chicago Institute of Art, which was part of the University of Chicago. "It was a marvelous experience," Ramona recalled. "In fact, one of my pictures hung in the Chicago Art Institute for many years."[25]

To unify the mission and communicate with the missionaries regularly, May produced a twenty-page monthly newsletter, the *Guide*. The June 1939 issue, one of the last issues before the Hinckleys completed their mission, was typical of the newsletter. Pictures of Bryant and May appeared on the cover under the title. Among the various messages and reports was a regular half-page column written by May to "the officers and members of the Relief Society of the Northern States Mission." As president of the mission's Relief Society, Primary, and YWMIA (by that time the name had been changed from Young Ladies' to Young Women's Mutual Improvement Association), May used this column to keep in contact with the leaders in the branches and to give them support.

"I only regret that I cannot come to each of you personally and express the love and appreciation that I hold in my heart for you my dear sisters who have worked so faithfully and so cheerfully with me in this organization," she wrote in June 1939. "I shall not forget you but shall cherish forever memories of the days spent with you in this mission. You have been so kind and gracious to me! You have won my enduring love. My successor will find a warm place in your hearts and you will give to her I am sure the same loyal and constant allegiance that you have given to me. May the Relief Society work forever claim your love and may your lives be enriched and ennobled through it." Then she closed with the three phrases that had become her trademark in every column: "Let us love. Let us serve. Let us work together."[26]

Serving as Third General Primary President

After serving for three and a half years, Bryant was released as mission president, and the Hinckleys returned to

Salt Lake City in July 1939. Since they had sold their home on Seventh South before leaving for Chicago, they lived with his daughter Ruth for about four months and then moved into the Belvedere Apartments in downtown Salt Lake City. Years earlier, Bryant had purchased a thirty-acre farm in the East Millcreek area of southeast Salt Lake City so that in the summers his children could experience the joy and work of rural life. The Hinckleys moved from their apartment into the family farm home. President Grant asked Bryant to be the secretary of education for the Church, and one of his duties was visiting seminaries all over the Church. With May's help, Bryant also wrote a book titled *Heber J. Grant, a Businessman,* and presented a series of radio broadcasts on KSL, *Religion in Everyday Life.*

On December 14, 1939, five months after the Hinckleys' return from Chicago, President Heber J. Grant called May Green Hinckley to serve as the third general president of the Primary. He told her, "May, we're going to give you 102,000 children,"[27] thus giving further meaning to the promise in her patriarchal blessing that she would be "mother to many children." She felt inadequate to accept the calling, but her husband encouraged her to try it, later noting that "she made a great Superintendent."[28]

The new presidency began serving on January 1, 1940. Adele Cannon Howells, who had been May's counselor in the Granite Stake YLMIA, served as first counselor for the entire term; Janet Lennox Murdock Thompson served as second counselor from January 1940 to May 1942 and was succeeded by LaVern Watts Parmley, who served in that position until May 1943. Eighteen women served on the general board, fifteen of whom had served under May's predecessor, May Anderson.

As one of their first endeavors, the new presidency commissioned a mural depicting the first Primary meeting in 1878. Lynn Fausett, a local artist, painted a mural for the rock meetinghouse in Farmington, Utah, where Primary began. Two great-great-grandchildren of Aurelia Spencer Rogers, the founder of that first ward Primary, unveiled the mural on August 24, 1941.

May chose a scripture as the theme of her administration: "And they shall also teach their children to pray, and to walk uprightly before the Lord" (D&C 68:28). The Primary introduced its seal and colors—the primary colors of red, yellow, and blue.[29] When Primary children sang, "Red is for courage to do what is right, Yellow for service from morning till night, Blue is for truth in our thought and our deed," they learned the significance of the Primary colors.[30]

In response to a survey of local Primary leaders, the implementation of the ward budget to finance auxiliaries, and the effects of World War II, the Primary presidency under May Hinckley simplified the Primary program and stressed more spiritual instruction. They reduced the number of ward activities to three a year—a spring Primary conference, a fall harvest festival, and a Christmas party. Each month's schedule for weekday Primary meetings included two meetings where lessons were taught, one lesson enrichment meeting, and an activity each month. Summer Primary focused on all-around development of children with arts and crafts, music, literature, dancing, citizenship training, and games.[31]

Classes underwent slight modifications: the Beginners (four- and five-year-olds) became Group I, and the next older class was named Group II. Seven- and eight-year-olds, known as Zion's Boys and Girls, were separated by age into two groups. The names of the older classes, the Trail Builders and the Home Builders, did not change.[32]

With her keen interest in the success of Primary in the missions, May organized a committee to write lessons for mission Primaries, which were published in the *Children's Friend*. Because of wartime gas rationing, home Primary replaced many Primary units in the mission field, and Primary leadership and conference meetings were eliminated, as was travel by general board members. To communicate with local leaders, the Primary published a quarterly bulletin and included a "June Conference by Mail" in the *Children's Friend*.[33]

One of May's responsibilities as president included supervising publication of the *Children's Friend*. She delegated the position of editor to her counselor, Adele Cannon Howells. Eager to encourage other people to develop their abilities, May invited people she knew who had artistic or literary potential to send contributions to the magazine. Ramona Hinckley was one who received such encouragement, and she appreciated the opportunity May gave her to have some of her artwork, a series of paper dolls, published in the *Children's Friend*.[34]

The Primary Children's Hospital, located on North Temple in the old Hyde home, was also under May's charge. She visited there every day and, because of her administrative experience at the medical clinic, efficiently kept it in operation. While her management of the hospital was businesslike, the atmosphere was warm and caring. Barbara Howells Moench, daughter of May's counselor Adele Howells, remembers going to the hospital to read to children and being impressed that the facility was "more of a home than a hospital."[35]

May usually carried with her a notebook which she filled with thoughts for talks. Typical of her entries are these: "Fundamental purposes never change." "Primary work should improve and brighten the lives of officers and teachers and build faith and character in the lives of the children. We touch and mold the lives of the children in more ways than by the spoken word. It is what we are that registers in their lives rather than what we say. Perfection cannot be expected of anyone but no conscientious Primary worker can make the contribution she should make unless in her heart and soul she subscribes to the requirement of the gospel and becomes an example to her associates and to the children."[36]

May's Final Days

Suffering acutely from arthritis, May entered the hospital for treatment in April 1943. Gordon, who was living nearby, drove her to the hospital. He recalled her being in "very low spirits" and telling him, "I don't want to go to the hospital. I've known enough of medicine that I know that that's where people go to die."[37] While she was in the hospital, she contracted pneumonia. Gordon remembered her doctor, with tears in his eyes, saying, "You study medicine all your life and at a time when you really need to help someone, you find yourself powerless."[38]

Just forty months after she was called to serve as Primary general president and only eleven years after her marriage to Bryant, May died the day after her sixty-second birthday, on May 2, 1943, with her husband and some of her family at her side. "When she died, it was a tragedy in our home," said Gordon. "I think of it now, the sorrow of that occasion."[39] Her funeral was held at the Assembly Hall on Temple Square.

May Green Hinckley's life had some setbacks and detours along the way, but she responded to each challenge in a cheerful and productive manner. She reached out to others, thinking of their needs rather than her own, and did so in a spirit of love, service, and working together. Her influence on her family, on the missionaries and members in the Northern States Mission, and on the Primary Association was profound. As one of the Hinckley daughters stated, "It was easy to love Aunt May."[40]

4

Adele Cannon Howells
1943–1951

Adele Cannon Howells, the fourth general president of the Primary, felt that material goods were to be shared with others. Throughout her life, she gave generously of her time and means, often expressing in her diary that she hoped she could do her "full part in building up the kingdom of God on this earth."[1] The Primary Children's Hospital, in particular, benefited not only from her large donations but also from her gracious personality, her persuasiveness in approaching others to contribute, and her administrative abilities in overseeing the planning and construction of a new, modern facility.

As important as her work in the Primary was Adele's work as a parent and grandparent. Although Adele and her husband, David, were not able to have children, they adopted three children and thus experienced firsthand the joys and challenges of parenthood. Determined to teach their children good, strong values, Adele and David, though financially blessed, taught them the value of work.

"There Goes a Man of God"

Adele's paternal great-grandparents, George and Ann Quayle Cannon, were living in Liverpool, England, when a young man, a brother-in-law they had never met, visited them. Several years earlier, George's sister Leonora had moved to

Canada, where she met and married John Taylor. After joining The Church of Jesus Christ of Latter-day Saints, John was called on a mission to England and, at his wife's request, sought out George and Ann. According to family history, Ann, after visiting with John, was so impressed with his demeanor and spirit that she told her son, "There goes a man of God. He is come to bring salvation to your father's house."[2] Later that evening, John, who would later serve as the third president of the Church, returned and began to teach the Cannons about the restored church. Both George and Ann were baptized in 1840, as were their three oldest children.

George spent the next two years saving money and making preparations to join the Saints in Nauvoo. Finally the Cannons, with their seven children (three children had died in infancy), sailed from Liverpool in 1842. Just more than a month later, Ann died at sea. Her bereaved husband and children arrived in Nauvoo in April 1843, and tragedy struck again the next year when George died of sunstroke.

Adele's grandfather, Angus Munn Cannon, the seventh of George and Ann's ten children, was only ten years old when his father died. He and his younger brothers and sister then lived with their oldest sister and her husband. When he was fifteen, Angus made the trek across the plains and, after arriving in the Salt Lake Valley, found work hauling wood and farming and later working as an apprentice at the *Deseret News*. Angus served a mission to the Eastern States, where he met the Mousley family in Centerville, Delaware.

In 1840, the same year that the Cannon family was introduced to the gospel in England, the Mousleys were taught by missionaries in Delaware. Ann McMenemy Mousley joined the Church along with several of her children, although her husband, Titus, did not. Although Titus never converted, he willingly agreed to his wife's desire for the family to move to Utah in 1857. After Angus completed his mission, he returned to Salt Lake City and became reacquainted with the Mousleys. He married two of their daughters, Sarah Maria and Ann Amanda, on the same day, July 18, 1858.

Brigham Young sent Angus and his family, among other

Saints, to form the Cotton Mission in southwestern Utah. Angus served as the first mayor of St. George and also as the marshal, butcher, mail carrier, and prosecuting attorney. His primary occupation, however, was ranching and raising cattle and horses. An expert horseman and trader, he enjoyed riding high-spirited animals, even in his later years, a trait that would be passed on to his granddaughter Adele Cannon. George Mousley Cannon, George and Sarah's son and Adele's father, was born on Christmas Day, 1861, in the campgrounds of what was then known as St. George Valley.

The Morrises, Adele's maternal ancestors, heard the message of the missionaries in their native Wales. John Morris, her great-grandfather, was born in Fodynban, Wales, in 1794. He married Barbara Thomas, from Talhairne, Wales, in 1814. In time they became the parents of ten children. John, Barbara, and four of their children joined the Church in 1849—with Elias, Adele's grandfather, the first of the family to be baptized in March of that year, and the others following over the next several months. Elias, who was twenty-four years old at the time, left Wales for Utah and in 1856, a few years after his arrival, married Mary Lois Walker, a convert from Leek, England. Their daughter, Marian Adelaide Morris, was born in Salt Lake City in 1861. She met George Mousley Cannon after his family moved back to Salt Lake City, and they were married on his birthday, December 25, 1884.

Childhood

Adele Morris Cannon, the eldest of George and Marian's nine children, was born January 11, 1886, in Salt Lake City, Utah. She had eight younger brothers and sisters: George M. Jr., Marian, Lucille, Jeanne, Vaughn, Nora, Lois, and Elias.

The Cannon home was located on Ashton Avenue and Seventh East, in an area known as Forest Dale, which, at the time, was a rural part of Salt Lake City. According to Adele's lifelong friend, Dessie Grant Boyle (whose father, Heber J. Grant, served as president of the Church from 1918 to 1945), the Cannons thus "enjoyed the amenities of town and country," with their spacious home and their yard, which had "shade trees, grass, flowers, fruit trees, a truck garden, and a stable."[3]

George Cannon, Adele's father, was, according to Dessie, "a person of great charm, . . . refined and gentle, a hard worker, and a good provider."[4] Active in the Church, a leader in the community, and one who loved nature, George initiated a project of planting numerous trees along the Salt Lake City streets. He served as the first president of the Utah State Senate.

Adele's mother, Marian, ran an efficient home and taught her children to take care of the needs of the home, including the washing, ironing, sewing, and baking because, Dessie said, she "abhorred dependence on tradesmen."[5] The girls learned to make preserves and to bottle and dry fruit. Marian served as the Relief Society president for many years, and her children learned through her example to reach out to others. People often came to the Cannon home for food or a meal or to receive comfort. Marian insisted that her children take music, dancing, art, or elocution lessons and that they practice diligently.

Dessie remembered Adele's home as a gathering place for the Cannon children's friends. She recalled that staying overnight "was an unforgettable experience, for there were many things to do and such good food to eat."[6] Marian usually baked hot raisin buns for her children to serve their guests.[7]

As a child, Adele suffered a bout of rheumatic fever, and the needed rest allowed her ample time to read—something she loved to do. According to an account in the *Children's Friend,* "When she was a girl she read so rapidly that her sisters liked to watch her turn the leaves as her eyes sped down the pages."[8] Adele attended Salt Lake City schools and graduated from the LDS High School and Business College in 1903. She completed a B.A. degree in physical education at the University of Utah in 1909, then taught English and physical education in Oakley, Idaho. Returning to Salt Lake City the next year, she became a physical education instructor at the LDS Business College and at the Deseret Gym. She also worked for the Salt Lake City recreation department, and in 1913, she published an article in the *Young Woman's Journal* on the playground movement. Adele served as a counselor to May Green, also a single woman, in the presidency of the Granite Stake YWMIA. The two women found that they worked well together and developed a friendship that would last a lifetime.

A Successful Marriage

David Parrish Howells, two years older than Adele, was born on March 19, 1884, to Thomas Francis and Mary Bratton Parrish Howells in Salt Lake City. He was the second of nine children. Because his schoolteacher father struggled to support his large family, David, at an early age, worked to supplement the family income. One of his first jobs was selling newspapers. Wanting to make Christmas more festive, he bought an apple for each one of his brothers and sisters one year with money he had earned.

With a diploma from the University of Utah in one hand and an engagement ring in the other, David proposed to Adele under the horse chestnut tree in the Cannons' yard in Forest Dale. On March 13, 1913, twenty-seven-year-old Adele and twenty-nine-year-old David were married. They moved to San Francisco, where he attended Hastings Law School.

Following his graduation, David formed a company that purchased movies made in the United States and distributed them in Europe, the Orient, Australia, New Zealand, and India. The business, a very successful financial venture, was entirely involved with silent movies, as "talkies" had not yet been invented. Adele served as David's secretary, and the two of them traveled extensively throughout the world. They maintained an apartment in New York City but spent much of their time abroad. During their travels, Adele acquired many treasures—rugs, furniture, china, books, and art. She had a good eye for art, and some of the paintings she purchased in Parisian art galleries for nominal sums were later worth considerably more. Adele served as the president of the Relief

Society and David as the branch president in New York. She was also a correspondent for the *Deseret News,* writing a column entitled "News from New York."

When David and Adele sold their film company in 1921, he suggested that she choose where they would live. He thought she would choose Paris, which she loved perhaps more than any other city in the world. However, she felt that it would be difficult to be active in the Church in Paris. Instead, she picked Los Angeles, for both the Church activity there and the warm climate.[9]

Although David graduated from law school, he never took the bar exam. Instead, he used his legal knowledge in his business endeavors. He started Western Costume Company, which provided costumes for many Hollywood productions. The Howells also bought controlling interest in the Neff Land and Livestock Company, renaming it Howells Livestock, Inc. They owned thousands of acres of grazing land in northern Utah as well as desert land in Juab County in central Utah. Their main ranch, which they named Thousand Peaks Ranch, was located on the Weber River in the Uintah Mountains in eastern Utah. They spent summers there, often with numerous guests. Adele loved the outdoors and especially horses, according to her friend Dessie, who observed, "She was never quite so happy as when riding on a mountain trail."[10]

In 1925, several years after their arrival in Los Angeles, David was called as bishop of the Adams Ward in the Los Angeles Stake. When the ward was later divided, he became the first bishop of the Wilshire Ward in the new Hollywood Stake. Adele was a devoted bishop's wife who shared in the joys and sorrows of the ward members by visiting the sick and bereaved, attending socials and programs with her husband, and entertaining in her home. Drawing upon these experiences, she wrote a series of articles for the *Improvement Era* in 1936 entitled "From the Diary of a Bishop's Wife." Her leadership skills were put to use through her service in the Relief Society and as the first president of the Hollywood Stake YWMIA.

David, at President Heber J. Grant's request, began a

search to select a site for a temple in the Los Angeles area. Harold Lloyd, an actor, owned a piece of property on Santa Monica Boulevard that David thought would be an appropriate setting for a temple. Through David's association with Bill Frazier, an uncle of the actor who handled his property, the Church acquired the lot in 1937. The Howells family contributed substantially to help finance the construction of the future temple. They also bought land next to the temple site and built two duplexes on it. One of Adele's fondest hopes was to see the Los Angeles Temple built so that she might work in it "in her old age."[11]

Home and Family

Adele and David longed to have children but were not able to. When they were in their late thirties, they adopted three children: Paul, Frances, and Barbara. The Howells's long-time housekeeper, Adele (Dede) Durtschi, helped Adele with the children and became part of the family. Dede, who had joined the Church in Switzerland as a young girl and immigrated to Utah, lived with the Howells family for the rest of Adele's life. Adele felt she had had her fill of the kitchen as the eldest of the nine Cannon children, so she turned most of the daily cooking over to Dede. Adele sometimes baked bread, which she gave to ward members and later to President Heber J. Grant and President George Albert Smith, and she enjoyed stirring up a batch of fudge on rainy days at the cabin in Utah.[12]

The Howells family lived in a home adjacent to the Wilshire Country Club. Barbara remembers, "We had a gorgeous home. All my friends went to private schools, but Daddy and Mother did not believe in that. I used to walk three miles to Los Angeles High School every morning. We had a gardener, yet I had to rake up the eucalyptus leaves every Saturday morning. They taught us how to work and so did Dede." Every summer the Howells family closed up their home in Los Angeles and moved to the ranch in Utah. Barbara recalled putting slipcovers over all the furniture "like the New Yorkers did."[13]

Barbara remembered her father as "a kind, sweet, good-looking man with white hair. We lived about seven miles from the Wilshire Ward, so I would wait for him in his car and read while he did his Church business. I remember his sense of humor and his kindness to all of the people who came to him as bishop." She also recalled that he liked to eat well, although it sometimes caused him problems with his ulcers. She asked him one day, "Daddy, why do you eat like this when it causes so much upset?" He replied, "I never had enough to eat as a child."[14]

As a young girl, Barbara especially enjoyed going with her father to visit his sisters in Utah. "Daddy had wonderful sisters. They all had a great sense of humor. As a family, the Howellses liked to laugh together and tell stories. I loved going to Kaysville to visit my aunt Margaret. Sitting in that kitchen in a country home was more fun for me than anything else. I envied my cousin because she had that kind of life on a farm."[15]

"Mother," Barbara said, "was refined and gracious. She never spoke ill of anyone. If something happened that was a crisis, she acted like it was nothing. It was Dede who told us we were adopted. But then people didn't talk openly about things like that."[16] Barbara felt she had "a wonderful life. I appreciate everything my mother did for me." One of her favorite memories is of wandering with her mother through her father's costume shop choosing costumes for the ward roadshows.[17]

"Addie," as most of her friends called Adele, was a gracious hostess and entertained often. President Heber J. Grant and his wife Augusta frequently stayed with the Howells family when they traveled to southern California. David and President Grant enjoyed golfing together. Notations of luncheons, dinners, and visiting fill many pages of Adele's diaries.

When David died suddenly in March 1939 of a heart attack at age fifty-five, Adele wrote in her diary: "The little lonely quail who has lost his mate is still in the garden. I can hear his plaintive call, 'I'm lonely, I want you, I love you.' But he is not as lonely as I." An avid diary keeper, Adele wrote many other pensive entries about missing her beloved companion, such as "I miss him more every day"; "I can't keep my mind off my terrible loss of David"; "Thinking much of Dave as always and wishing he were here—the ranch is beautiful."[18] Barbara noted, "Daddy was the love of her life."[19] But Adele, who knew she must press on, expressed gratitude for her children and her other blessings and hoped that she would bear her lot "with patience and good cheer." She also found later as she became immersed in Primary that this calling was an unforeseen blessing. Adele wrote, "What a Godsend work is! I'm so busy I have not time to think about myself and how lonesome I am."[20]

After David's death, as she was contemplating whether to stay in Los Angeles or return to Salt Lake City, she received a call to serve as a counselor to her old friend May Green Hinckley, who had just been called as the third Primary general president. Although Adele had never served in the Primary, she felt that this new call was an answer to her prayers. She and her children moved to Salt Lake City, and Adele began her work in the Primary on January 1, 1940. She turned the operation of the ranches over to her brother-in-law, Ira Sharp, but maintained an active involvement in managing the business.

In the Primary Presidency

Adele was set apart as first counselor in the Primary general presidency by President J. Reuben Clark Jr., a counselor in the First Presidency. Of her blessing she recorded in her diary, "It was a fine satisfaction. I hope I can do this work as it should be done."[21]

Because of Adele's writing talents, May appointed her editor of the *Children's Friend*. Adele determined to improve both its quality and the number of subscriptions. She adopted the slogan "Good Reading for Children" and initiated pages for children's art and also hands-on activities such as paper dolls and cutouts—no doubt remembering her own childhood love of reading and art. She started the "Exchange Page," a forum for Primary workers to share ideas, and "In Your Own Corner," a page for children to describe items they had created at home. She requested children to write about their hobbies and pets. To encourage them to keep a journal and to understand the pioneer experience, she printed excerpts from pioneer diaries. [22]

Because of the paper shortages caused by World War II, one of the challenges of publishing the magazine was obtaining enough paper each month to print it. Several times, Adele and the priesthood advisers appealed to the United States government for permission to obtain more paper, which was being rationed. Once when the general board was notified that the *Children's Friend* had been granted twenty-eight extra tons of paper, the members celebrated at their weekly meeting.

Adele's service with May came to an end just three years after they were called as a presidency. When May became seriously ill and was hospitalized, Adele visited May often in the hospital. Following her friend's death in May 1943, Adele paid for her hospital expenses.[23] She wrote in her diary, "It poured rain during the night as if nature was weeping for May's death. . . . I have said good-bye to one of my dearest friends."[24]

Serving As Fourth General President

Two months later, on July 19, Adele received a telephone call from President David O. McKay of the First Presidency, who said that President Grant wished to see her that day. When she was ushered into the Church president's office, President Grant shook her hand and then, she said, "kissed me as he would his own daughter." Adele was indeed almost a daughter to President Grant. When she and Dessie had become friends as young teenagers, she had spent many happy hours in the Grant home. A warm friendship had continued between Adele and President Grant even after she was married, and the Grants had often been guests in her home in California. Adele's calling to serve in the Primary presidency provided many opportunities for her to meet with President Grant again. (When he died on May 14, 1945, she felt a great sense of loss and wrote, "Last night I saw one of the most beautiful sights I have ever seen. The spires of the temple were illuminated and in the sky behind it was the crescent with a star I have never seen before near one tip. I couldn't help thinking of President Grant and that this was a new star in heaven."[25])

While she met with President Grant that summer day in 1943, he extended to her a call to serve as the fourth Primary general president. Recalling the events of that afternoon, she wrote, "I replied that I would be pleased to do so if they thought I was capable of doing it well and would do everything in my power to fill the office satisfactorily."[26] Adele, who by now had three years service in the Primary, brought to this calling an understanding of various cultures and conditions from living and traveling in many parts of the world as well as a great desire to help children develop in many areas of their lives.

She chose as her counselors LaVern Watts Parmley and her lifelong friend, Dessie Grant Boyle, both of whom would serve with her for her entire term. When the new Primary presidency began serving in the summer of 1943, they released all the general board members who had been on the board for ten years or more but retained the sixteen members who had served less than ten years. Adele restructured curriculum development and asked general board members, rather than institute teachers, to write lesson manuals because she felt they knew children better.

In keeping with one of Adele's favorite slogans, "Busy Days Are Happy Days," and her own love of art and animals, she encouraged children to have hobbies, to participate in arts and crafts, and, if possible, to have pets. She displayed children's art and handiwork in her office. She also privately established scholarship funds at Brigham Young University and the University of Utah training schools to develop art skills in children.

Adele became president of the Primary during World

War II, a time that had a great impact on both children and the Primary program. Because many parents were involved in the war, with fathers serving in the military and mothers working outside the home, a number of Primary children were often without adequate adult supervision and support. Thus, Adele felt that Primary should play an even more important role in children's lives.[27] Because of wartime travel restrictions, home and neighborhood Primary meetings were held in many areas of the Church. Lessons written for these smaller organizations, as well as Primary meetings held in mission areas, were published in the *Children's Friend*.[28] At the end of the war, Adele asked Primary children in the United States to help Primary children in war-torn Europe. Week after week children brought toys they chose to donate and clothing they had outgrown—to be shipped by the Church to Germany, England, France, and Holland. The donations not only assisted Saints who had lost so much during the war, but the donors themselves also learned the spirit of giving.

Two years after her call as president, Adele reflected on her Primary service in her diary. "Anniversary of my appointment as president of the Primary Association," she wrote. "I am enjoying the work immensely and hope I am doing some good."[29]

The Howells family's experiences in their film business had helped Adele become familiar with the far-reaching influence of mass media. *Children's Friend of the Air,* a fifteen-minute radio program that began June 15, 1946, was a culmination of Adele's efforts to broadcast programming for children that was uplifting and gospel-oriented. In 1947, for the centennial of the arrival of the Saints in the Salt Lake Valley, she suggested that Primary children plant trees as "living memorials to the pioneers"—perhaps following her father's example. Primary children were also asked to donate nickels to a fund to help erect a "This Is the Place" Monument at the mouth of Emigration Canyon, honoring the July 1847 arrival of the pioneers in the Salt Lake Valley. This was another opportunity for children to learn to give. The fund also provided money to support the Primary Children's Hospital and to commission three murals by Lee Greene Richards for the baptismal area of the Idaho Falls Temple; the murals were indicative of Adele's constant desire to enrich through art.

In 1948, shortly after television was introduced in Utah, the Primary sponsored *Junior Council,* a half-hour weekly show on which a panel of children answered questions submitted by the studio audience and by readers of the *Children's Friend.* Adele's influence in the program is clear: it included demonstrations of art, music, crafts, and nature projects, a "Be Kind to Animals Club," and entertainment that included puppet shows, musical numbers, and plays.[30]

Knowing the value of art as a teaching tool, Adele had felt for years that children would be better able to understand the Book of Mormon if beautiful pictures accompanied simplified stories. Under her direction, the Primary commissioned artist Arnold Friberg to paint a series of Book of Mormon illustrations in 1950. The pictures, along with a narrative prepared by a general board member, were scheduled to appear in the *Children's Friend* in 1952 as part of the Primary's celebration of the fiftieth anniversary of the magazine. The artworks have since become well known to Church members everywhere. Adele initiated a campaign to increase subscriptions to the magazine to fifty thousand by the Jubilee year.

Adele also encouraged music as a teaching tool. *The Children Sing,* a new songbook published in 1951, was compiled by a committee that included members of the Junior Sunday School and the Primary general boards. More than two dozen new songs focusing on gospel principles were composed for the book.

At Primary conference in 1951, a two-day gathering of Primary workers held prior to April general conference, the presidency hosted a breakfast at the Hotel Utah to honor stake Primary presidents. An evening testimony meeting for Primary leaders was held at the Assembly Hall. Gold loving cups were given to all stakes that over a three-year-period had met a certain level of subscriptions to the *Children's Friend.*

An able executive and businesswoman, Adele was effective in her relationships with others, and she thoroughly

enjoyed meeting and working with people. Because the major-
ity of Church members in the 1940s lived in the Western
United States, she was able to personally meet with many local
Primary leaders as well as to visit various stakes. For example,
Adele made a note in her diary of the whole presidency
attending the Ensign stake board meeting at the stake Primary
president's home. "It is always a pleasure for me to meet such
fine devoted women," Adele noted. Adele thought of herself
as a Primary worker and didn't mind helping out even when
she was the guest of honor. After presenting diplomas to thirty
graduating Primary boys and girls at a dinner in Yalecrest
Ward, in Salt Lake City, she wrote, "I helped with the dishes
and clearing up. It was very inspiring to see so many fine
young boys and girls complete their Primary work."[31]

Adele found respite from her demanding schedule by
visiting the ranch, which she called the "House with No
Secrets." Frequent guests for evening or weekend visits
included her counselors, general board members, General
Authorities, and other friends. She often invited the ranch
hands to join her guests for dinner and made them feel a part
of her circle of friends.

She enjoyed horseback riding at the ranch so much that
she continued to ride even as her health began to fail. Two of
her favorite horses she named Primary and Friend.

Once Adele asked her son-in-law Lorin Moench, a pilot,
to fly her to the ranch so that she could see it from the air. He
recalled that "she was very observant and wanted to see all the
areas she had seen by horseback and by hiking. It was quite
challenging to land under those circumstances, on the small
strip at the head of the Weber River, but she was very calm
and a good sport. After we landed, she proudly told us that for
the past forty years she had come up to the ranch by all means
of transportation. She had walked up, gone by horseback, covered wagon, railroad, automobile—and now by plane."[32]

Adele had a strong testimony of the gospel and
expressed her feelings in short statements such as these:
"Rereading Grandma Morris' diary, a very remarkable docu-
ment. She repeatedly tells of her faith in the gospel. I have the

same testimony of its truthfulness although I do not speak of it so often. . . . I believe in the Church as never before and want to do my full part and hope my children will also!"[33]

"Buy a Brick"

One of Adele's major responsibilities as Primary president was administering Primary Children's Hospital and serving as president of the board of trustees. She was well suited for this task. In 1938, architect George Cannon Young began preparing plans for a new hospital to replace the convalescent home on North Temple. The First Presidency, under President Grant, formally authorized the new hospital in 1939, but fund raising and planning were halted when World War II broke out.

After the war, President George Albert Smith, who succeeded President Grant, renewed authorization, and the Primary moved forward on building the hospital, which would be larger and more costly than the one originally planned. A site was selected at Twelfth Avenue and D Street, on a hillside northeast of downtown Salt Lake City.

Primary leaders proposed many creative ways to raise money for the project. For years, children had donated birthday pennies to the old hospital. In addition, to help them feel that they had part in the construction of the new hospital, Adele suggested that for each dime contributed, they could "buy a brick." This campaign raised more than twenty thousand dollars.

Ground-breaking ceremonies were held in April 1949 during Primary conference. One year later, the cornerstone was laid. Mementos placed in the cornerstone box included several historical documents and a list of the names of the children who had donated their dimes to buy bricks.[34] One young boy, excited that he had been able to contribute, told his parents as they drove past the new building, "See that hospital? Well, I helped build it. One of my bricks is right there somewhere in that wall!"[35] Adele was no doubt pleased that the Primary children were experiencing the same joy of giving that she had often felt.

A Devoted Grandmother

Since Paul, Frances, and Barbara and their families lived in Salt Lake City, Adele could see her grandchildren frequently. Paul's son, the first grandchild, was named after his grandfather, David. A devoted grandmother, she often took care of her grandchildren. "I had a great time tending them," she wrote in her diary. "They are adorable."[36] Other entries typified her feelings for her family: "Barbara and Lorin came home for supper bringing the baby. We all spent the evening here and had a very happy time. It is glorious to have my family. . . . I love my children and my grandchildren most dearly and hope they will all live the gospel."[37] A long-held family tradition was gathering at Adele's home for Christmas Eve dinner. Many times she took her grandchildren to church with her and sat with them in Junior Sunday School. Usually the teachers were unaware that she was the Primary general president.

Adele kept in touch with her family in many ways and often telephoned her extended family members to see how they were faring. In her diary, she noted frequent get-togethers with David's family and hers. Her son-in-law Lorin observed that she always was "calm, collected, and in control. I don't think I ever heard her raise her voice." Adele's trait of typically remaining calm in a crisis was especially evident once when she flew with Lorin and several others to southern California. Just as they began to descend into the Los Angeles basin, fog started to roll in from the ocean, and the radio and lights in his surplus navy plane went out. He could not make contact with ground control nor did he have any navigational equipment. But, he recalled, Adele "just sat there relaxed and said everything would be OK. She never got riled."[38]

Honors and Community Service

Adele loved to act on her belief that material blessings were a means to helping others, and she gave generously to individuals, charities, and organizations. At Easter and Christmas, she purchased clothing and other items and packed boxes to give to needy families. Parking lot attendants, her hairdresser, and many others who helped her received gifts of appreciation—frequently a package of lamb chops. Friends and family members often received Church books, usually inscribed by the authors at Adele's request.

She noted in her diary in February 1944, "I made quite substantial gifts to the Church this week in the form of Utah-Idaho common stock (sugar company). I allotted equal parts to the building fund of the Children's Hospital, the genealogical departments . . . and a student loan fund at the BYU. . . . As I have told the children ever since Dave's death, I do not intend to give them a fortune. They will be given plenty for their urgent needs. If they work hard enough, they can succeed as well as Dave did. We must not keep everything for our own comfort."[39]

Adele was elected to the Salt Lake City Hall of Fame in 1948, although she was reluctant to accept that honor until President George Albert Smith urged her to do so, saying it would bring honor to the Primary and to the Church.

Adele's Legacy of Service

By 1951, Adele had been ailing for a time, but because she did not want her associates and friends to be concerned, she asked her son-in-law, Lorin, to fly her to California to see a physician. The doctor removed fluid from her lungs, but they kept filling with more fluid. She returned to Salt Lake City two weeks later with her daughter Barbara. In a poignant moment before her death, she told Barbara, "I have one regret—that I didn't have more to do with you and Frances as you were growing up."[40] The rheumatic fever she had as a child had weakened her heart, and she died at age sixty-five on April 14, 1951, only days after delivering an address in the Tabernacle for Primary general conference and "'in the harness,' as she had hoped," according to her friend Dessie Boyle.[41] Following funeral services held in the Assembly Hall on Temple Square, she was buried in Forest Lawn Memorial Park in Los Angeles beside her beloved David.

Adele did not live to see many of her dreams realized, but she left behind a legacy of service. The new Primary Children's Hospital was completed and dedicated nine months after her death. The Los Angeles Temple was dedicated by President David O. McKay in 1956, nineteen years after her husband had facilitated purchase of the property. The first Arnold Friberg Book of Mormon painting appeared in the *Children's Friend* in 1953, one year after the magazine's jubilee. However, by 1952, Adele's campaign to obtain fifty thousand subscriptions for the fiftieth anniversary had been so successful that the number mounted to seventy-two thousand. Although she could not experience their fulfillment, the goals she helped initiate, plan, and support have blessed the lives of thousands of Church members, especially the children whom she served with love and devotion.

5

LaVern Watts Parmley

1951–1974

*T*hat LaVern Watts Parmley was the first woman to serve on a national committee of the Boy Scouts of America and the first woman to receive Scouting's highest honor, the Silver Buffalo, is not at all surprising. Throughout her life, she felt "the Lord was . . . preparing [her] to be a leader of boys."[1] Not only a leader of boys in the Scouting program, she was also a dynamic president, who, in addition to administering the general Primary programs, supervised the completion of the new Primary Children's Hospital in 1952, served as chairman of the board of trustees of the hospital, and worked as editor of the *Children's Friend.*

Being one of eleven children, most of them boys, LaVern developed leadership skills early in life. She and her husband, Tom, had three children—two boys and a girl. She considered boys her "specialty" and worked tirelessly to improve the Church's programs for young boys. This dedication, coupled with her energy and excellent health throughout her long term of service as Primary general president, distinguish her as a great friend to children of the Church.

A Pioneer Heritage

LaVern's pioneer heritage was filled with examples of strong faith and commitment to the gospel of Jesus Christ. Her great-grandfather William Park, born at Cambuslang, Scotland, October 26, 1805, immigrated to Canada in 1820. There he married a Scottish woman, Jane Duncan, in 1828. LDS missionaries taught them the gospel, and they were baptized in 1844 at Warwick, Canada. The Parks joined the Saints in Winter Quarters, Nebraska, in 1846, and the following spring began their trek to the Salt Lake Valley, arriving October 2, 1847, and settling in the Mill Creek area in the southeast part of the valley. LaVern's grandfather, Andrew Duncan Park, was one of their eleven children.

Jane, a midwife, was a counselor in the Relief Society in Mill Creek. Her granddaughter Jane Park Hulse remembered that she was "a woman of strong personality and amiable disposition," not unlike LaVern, and "doing much good among the sick in the early pioneer days."[2] She left twenty-five dollars to each granddaughter named after her—money she had saved from her earnings as a midwife.

LaVern's maternal grandmother, Jane Ann Ellison Park, was born in Parr, Lancashire, England, in 1849. Her parents, James and Alice Halliwell Ellison, joined the Church and immigrated with their six children to Utah in 1853. They lived first in Kaysville and then in Nephi, where James helped build a fort to protect the town from hostile Indians. After Jane married Andrew Duncan Park in 1868, they lived in Mill Creek, where she served as a Relief Society teacher and as Primary president. "She was especially kind to the sick and those who were less fortunate than she and never cared for show or honor," wrote her daughter Jane Hulse.[3] Gertrude Park, LaVern's mother, was the sixth of Jane and Andrew Duncan Park's nine children.

LaVern's paternal grandparents, George C. and Rebecca Bawden Watts, were both born in Moulton, Devonshire, England. Rebecca's parents joined the Church in England in 1848 and immigrated to Utah a few years later with their three small children. Rebecca married George September 14, 1867, and their son William Eugene (Gene) Watts was LaVern's father.

Gertrude Park met Gene at the Union Dance Hall in

Midvale. After a short courtship, sixteen-year-old Gertrude and twenty-two-year-old Gene were married November 10, 1897, in Salt Lake City. The couple lived in a duplex near the Murray smelter where Gene worked. After the births of their first two children, they bought a fifteen-acre farm in Murray so that Gene would not have to work in the polluted environment of the smelter and so they would have a home and farm for their family. Realizing that the farm could not totally support his growing family, Gene found employment at the Utah-Idaho Sugar Company in West Jordan, twelve miles southwest of Murray. Although small in stature, he was energetic and articulate and soon became the negotiator between the sugar company and the sugar beet farmers. He raised sugar beets himself on most of his acreage.

The Watts Family Weathers the Depression

Martha LaVern Watts was born in Murray, Utah, "the first day of the new century, January 1, 1900, of which she was utterly proud."[4] One of her brothers later commented that the family reckoned time by her birth date.[5] Until she was fifteen years old, when her sister Beryl was born, LaVern was raised in a family of boys. She was the second child and first daughter of Gertrude and Gene's eleven children, who also included Denzil, Cloris, Merlin, Blaine, John, Stanley, Beryl Jean, Maurice, Helen June, and Wendell. Because her mother had poor health most of her life and LaVern was the eldest daughter, she was like a second mother to her siblings and, as a result, developed at a young age a remarkable ability to handle children, especially boys.

Especially when a new brother or sister joined the Watts family, LaVern assumed additional responsibilities in taking care of her brothers and sisters. But she made sure that her brothers did their share of the work as well. She put the boys to work helping with the family wash. The hand-cranked washer was set up under a tree in the yard, and with the other boys counting, each boy had to turn the crank one hundred times.[6] She was a strict disciplinarian: later her husband, Tom

Parmley, would comment, "Well do the younger ones in the family remember the long half hours spent sitting disconsolately on the straight hard-backed kitchen chairs in punishment for snitching some freshly baked cake."[7]

Just two weeks after her first sister, Beryl, was born, LaVern became seriously ill with appendicitis and had to have surgery. Her mother moaned, "We just get another girl, and now we're going to lose our first one."[8] Fortunately, the operation was successful, and fifteen-year-old LaVern returned home to enjoy her new baby sister as well as to continue helping her mother.

Perhaps because she had so many new babies to tend throughout her childhood and because she had a natural rapport with boys, LaVern said, "I spent very little time with dolls. . . . I loved to play football, basketball, and handball. We had a basketball standard and hoop in the back yard and there was a game going on constantly."[9] She kept up with her brothers not only in sports but also in farm work. "I used to go out and weed beets with the rest of the boys," she remembered in an interview. "We had a garden. We had an orchard and I used to get the salt shaker and go out in the apple tree and eat green apples and read books. I loved to read. I've always loved to read any book that I could find."[10] Her favorite book was *Anne of Green Gables* by Lucy Maud Montgomery.

The Watts children earned extra money by selling tomatoes they raised for fifty cents a bushel. But they didn't spend all their time working, for LaVern said, "We used to have more fun sleighriding. Dad was always very generous. If any young people wanted a team of horses, they knew they could come to him. We ice skated on an old pond that would freeze up. We would build a fire on the side."[11] Stan, a brother, commented, "Mom bought a piano and taught LaVern to play it. We used to have family home evening and sing around the piano. We spent most of our time together as a family because we were too poor to go anywhere."[12]

"My daddy liked to dance and my grandmother loved to dance," LaVern recalled. "We always used to go to the dances, and he would dance with Grandmother, his mother. Then he would always dance with me and so I thought he was very special."[13] Grandmother Watts, who was then a widow, lived next door. "Often I would sleep with Grandma," LaVern remembered, "and she did a lot of knitting. Particularly at night when she couldn't sleep, she would knit stockings with these steel needles, and I could hear them clicking nearly all night long."[14] When LaVern stayed with her, Grandma Watts sometimes served LaVern's favorite foods—fried potatoes and green tomato pickles.

Gene, while a baptized Mormon, did not feel that church attendance and activity were necessary. From him the children learned the "value of being a good neighbor, and the importance of honesty, integrity, and unselfishness,"[15] LaVern said. "He wasn't too active in the Church and he smoked, but I don't think anyone had a better father. He loved us. He would do anything in the world for us."[16] LaVern's brother Maurice, or Nick, as he was called, said, "Dad was a farmer most of his life. He was a small, wiry guy, a hard worker with lots of energy and a good sense of humor. He was very kind and gentle to all of us kids but demanding. He would say, 'OK, Maurice, you have eight rows of beets to thin today, and Wen, you've got six rows, and Stan, you've got ten rows to thin.' We knew when he came home that they'd better be thinned."[17]

Gertrude remained active in the Church, and while she served as a counselor and secretary in the Relief Society, LaVern often helped her with her books and records. Gertrude was also a counselor in the Primary and taught religion class. Nick Watts remembered his mother making eight loaves of bread a day on a coal-burning stove to feed their family of eleven children and her heating water on Saturday nights for baths.[18] Though she worked hard to sustain her family through those difficult Depression years and though material goods were scarce, Gertrude's love of beauty was apparent to her children. "Mother loved flowers," LaVern recalled, "and she always had lovely flowers in her garden. She loved cosmos."[19]

The Watts family lived in the Grant Ward of the Cottonwood Stake, which at that time covered the communities of Murray, Taylorsville, and Cottonwood. LaVern remembered riding the streetcar with her family to every stake meeting. She attended Liberty Elementary School and graduated with the first class of Murray High School, where she was involved in drama, ballet, and chorus and was on the newspaper staff.

Although LaVern was anxious to go to college, she knew her parents couldn't afford it. Two weeks before she graduated from high school, the superintendent, who recognized her maturity and ability to work with young people, offered her a teaching job and told her that if she would go to summer school, she could have a contract. She wondered if he knew she was only a high school senior. He responded, "We've been watching you and know you can do it."[20] Thus, she taught during the school year and then went to summer school for the next six years. She didn't graduate but did obtain a two-year teaching certificate, which qualified her for the contract.

Newlyweds in New York

LaVern met Thomas Jennison Parmley at Saltair, a resort on the shore of the Great Salt Lake, where she had gone with her family and friends on a ward outing. Tom was there with a group of friends. Tom and LaVern enjoyed each other's company that day but didn't meet again for some time. The next opportunity arose when her ward sponsored an outing in Big Cottonwood Canyon and one of the boys invited Tom to go along. Tom and LaVern paired off and hiked all day, the beginning of a three-year courtship.

Tom was born November 2, 1897, in Scofield, Utah. After his father was killed in a mine accident, his mother supported her family as a seamstress. She advised her six children to stay active in the Church and to get a good education. When Tom was in the fifth grade, his family moved from Scofield to a one-acre farm in Sandy. Besides helping with family farm chores, he earned money by picking berries or unloading mining cars full of ore. Following his mother's advice, he obtained a bachelor's degree in physics at the University of Utah.

LaVern and Tom were married June 28, 1923, in the Salt

Lake Temple. Because married women were not allowed to teach, LaVern had to resign her position. However, two weeks after school started that fall, the principal at Ensign Elementary School, where she had most recently taught, called her to substitute, and she ended up teaching the whole year. Perhaps her effectiveness as a teacher was due in part to her experiences in teaching and disciplining her brothers, for she said of her teaching days, "I always felt I had a good rapport with children and we worked well together. I have never really had what I would call real discipline problems with my youngsters when I taught school."[21]

In 1924, the Parmleys moved to Ithaca, New York, where Tom pursued a Ph.D. in physics at Cornell University. Relocating was a great adventure for LaVern; until she married, she had been out of Salt Lake City only once, on a trip to Idaho. At Cornell LaVern worked in the alumni office, where her responsibilities included locating missing alumni, which she thought was a lot like doing genealogy. Because of her determination to find graduates, she was put in charge of that area of the alumni office and worked there until Tom received his degree.

LaVern and Tom enjoyed living in New York. They attended all the Cornell home football games and spent one summer sightseeing on the East Coast. Since Ithaca is close to Palmyra, they often went to the Joseph Smith Sr. farm and the Hill Cumorah and took all their visitors there.

When the Parmleys moved to Ithaca, the only other Church members there were students—a half dozen couples from the West. A branch of the Church had not yet been organized, so the small group of Latter-day Saints held Sunday School each week in Barnes Hall, a campus building designated for religious use. LaVern taught Sunday School.

In Ithaca, LaVern and Tom made many friends, both among members of the Church and people of other faiths. The LDS students and their spouses shared Thanksgiving dinners. The Parmleys lived in a large home that had been converted into apartments. Two other Latter-day Saint couples lived there also. When one of the couples was a little too eager to convert the landlady, she told the Parmleys, "Now, we like you, but just talk to us when we ask questions. We don't like people to force their religion on us." Others told them, "You have made more friends here because you lived your religion and you talked to us when we wanted to know about it, but you weren't always pushing it and making us feel that we were obligated."[22]

A compatible couple, LaVern and Tom loved to be together, but when LaVern became homesick after two years of living away from Utah, Tom suggested that she travel to Utah for a visit. Two weeks later, the telephone rang and it was Tom. LaVern was indeed surprised, but pleased, when he told her he was at the train station in Salt Lake City. After a few weeks longer in Utah, they returned to New York for Tom's final year at Cornell.

Family Fun

After Tom received his Ph.D., he obtained a teaching position at the University of Utah, and he and LaVern moved back to Salt Lake City. They became the parents of three children: Ellen Frances (Frannie), born April 16, 1929; Richard Thomas, born February 5, 1932; and William Watts, born January 22, 1936. "All our children were very active," said LaVern. "We had basketball hoops and volleyball nets up, and our home was always filled with our children's friends."[23] Often LaVern and Tom joined in the athletic activities. Frannie remembered her mother as "a pretty good athlete. Mother really loved sports. We used to go to all the football and basketball games at the University of Utah."[24]

The Parmleys took many vacations together; Richard's favorite vacations were family trips to Yellowstone.[25] The family also owned a cabin in Emigration Canyon, east of the city, which Bill thought was "absolutely spectacular. We went up a lot of weekends and occasionally would stay as long as a week during the summer. It had a natural spring—the best water I have ever tasted."[26]

Later, as their children married and had children, LaVern

and Tom enjoyed their thirteen grandchildren. "Mother was a terrific grandmother," Frannie said. "Mother and Dad took my daughters to Disneyland and my boys to the Philmont Scout Ranch in New Mexico. They were with us on holidays. On Christmas Eve, they stayed until the children went to bed, and then came back [to] our house by the time they woke up. They were very much involved with the family."[27]

Tom commented about some of LaVern's personal qualities: "She was extremely level-headed. She learned to hold her own with boys. She was never overwhelmed or overly concerned. She was an engine in motion. The mental picture I have of LaVern is of a woman with a bag in her hands coming home from a trip. She could drive but she seldom drove a car. She never had to worry about it because she could always find someone to take her."[28]

Vickie Muir Stewart, the eldest grandchild, remembers going to her grandparents' home nearly every Sunday for dinner. "Grandma always had the same menu, and we loved it. To this day, when I smell leg of lamb, I think of her unfailingly. Her icebox rolls were really, really good," said Vickie. "I always felt that there was a safety net under my family because of my grandparents.

"My grandmother was not a person who spoke about her feelings. I never recall having a conversation with her where deep feelings were expressed. Her diaries have nothing in them that indicate any emotion; they are simply records of her activities."[29]

According to LaVern's brother Nick, Tom and LaVern complemented each other: she was matter-of-fact and serious while Tom had a good sense of humor. Her sister Beryl noted, "They were very loving. Tom always praised LaVern. Anything she did was just wonderful. Whenever they invited us to a dinner, Tom would be the first to compliment her on how well everything was cooked and prepared, 'Just wonderful, LaVern, just wonderful.' She expressed a lot of love to him, too."[30] She was involved in Tom's university activities, participating in the University Women's Club and other university groups and helping him chaperone fraternity events. One of their favorite associations was membership in a Church history club. Since two other couples in the club had cabins near the Parmleys, many gatherings were held in the canyon. The children of the couples became friends, and some of them later formed their own Church history group.

Remembering her own urgent desire to obtain a college education, LaVern helped her younger brothers and sisters to obtain theirs. Beryl and Nick both lived with Tom and LaVern when they attended the University of Utah, and they, in turn, often helped the Parmleys by taking care of the children when LaVern had to be away from home on Church assignments.

LaVern was considerate and kind to other people. Besides dozens of cookies, she gave loaves of apple and banana bread to friends and neighbors. She stitched needlepoint pieces for general board members. When she heard about a woman who sent a card every day to someone she wasn't able to visit in person, LaVern adopted the idea and mailed a card to someone every day. She believed that no one could be too busy to think about others. Tom remembered buying postage stamps by the rolls.

LaVern's Specialty

From the time LaVern was in her teens, she held responsible positions in the Church. At age fourteen, she taught a Sunday School class. Within the next few years, she also taught in Primary and the YWMIA, was secretary to the ward choir, and was principal of the religion class, the program initiated in 1890 to supplement children's Sunday religious instruction. Both Primary and religion class were held on weekday afternoons; Primary provided activities for children while religion class presented gospel lessons for older children. As principal, LaVern supervised the organization and teaching in her ward's religion class.

Following the Parmleys' return to Salt Lake City from Ithaca, LaVern was called to serve on the Bonneville Stake Primary board in 1938. The stake Primary president assigned her the boys' program, which LaVern said was her "specialty."

Marion G. Romney, her stake president, set her apart and in that blessing told her, "You are a woman with a special capacity, and you will do an even greater work than you have ever done."[31]

Three years later, in July 1941, LaVern received a call to serve on the Primary general board, where her first major assignment was to revise the boys' program. When she first went out of town for Primary general board assignments, she traveled by train or bus. Tom said to her, "How I remember the many times I have taken you down to the depot to put you on the train to go!"[32] Later, when commercial airline travel became more common, LaVern and other Primary leaders began to travel by plane.

In February 1942, just seven months after her call to the general board, LaVern was called as second counselor to general president May Green Hinckley and was designated adviser to the Trail Builders and the Cub Scout programs. In July 1943, she was named first counselor to Adele Cannon Howells, who succeeded May Hinckley as general president. President David O. McKay of the First Presidency set her apart for that position. She later recalled in the blessing she was promised that she "was the one the Lord wanted" in the position and that she "should do away with all her fears."[33]

Her youngest child, Bill, was five years old when she began her general Primary service. Memories of their growing-up years are filled with Primary. On Thursday nights, general board nights, Frannie and Tom fixed dinner for the family, which Frannie recalled as "a good learning experience for me. Mother had things well organized, believe me!"[34] Richard enjoyed his mother's involvement, particularly in Scouts. He quite frequently went to the Deseret Gym to work out and dropped in at the Primary offices afterwards.[35] Bill also "hung out" at her office, usually taking a book to read. "I remember her being in the office a lot of time," he said. "I do remember one trip on the train with her to Idaho to a conference—just the two of us. We rode on a sleeper, and I took a model airplane to work on."[36]

The Fifth Primary General President

Adele Howells died April 14, 1951. A few weeks later, President McKay extended to LaVern the call to serve as fifth Primary general president. Though she had been Adele's first counselor, she had never expected to be called as president. "I felt very humble because it was a tremendous responsibility. . . . But President McKay was so gracious to me and he felt that I was the one the Lord wanted. . . . I had never thought that the time would come when I would be in the presidency and then to be president! I often say, 'That little country girl, what's she doing up there?' "[37]

The new Primary presidency was announced on May 16, 1951. LaVern chose Arta M. Hale as her first counselor and Florence H. Richards as her second counselor. At the time, there were 180 stake Primary organizations in the Church and 157,000 Primary children enrolled. Seven women served as LaVern's counselors during her twenty-three-year administration. When Sister Richards was released in June 1953, Leone W. Doxey became second counselor. She was followed by Eileen R. Dunyon in April 1962, Lucile C. Reading in July 1963, and Florence R. Lane in January 1970. When Sister Hale was released in April 1962, Sister Doxey became first counselor. She was followed by Sister Reading in January 1970 and Naomi W. Randall in October 1970.

"President Marion G. Romney always says he trained me," LaVern said after she was called as president. "He was my bishop in the Thirty-third Ward. . . . He was also my stake president. And then when I went on the general board, he was my adviser. Now he is in the First Presidency."[38]

During LaVern's administration, the general board was comprised of seventy strong and capable women. Trilba Lindsay, who served as a general board member and general secretary of the Primary, commented, "LaVern had high expectations of the board members. Some might have feared her just a little bit because of the strong demand, but it was that little bit of fear that helped them to perform up to her expectations."[39] Board meetings were held on Thursday afternoons and often extended into the evenings. LaVern fasted each Thursday to prepare herself spiritually.

"She was a great follower and advocate of our priesthood advisers," Trilba said. "She would rarely make a move of any import without consulting them. All she did was with the child in mind. Her question always was, What is best for the child? How can we at this level get down to children through appropriate channels? She loved those who had gone before her and built on the great work and foundation that had been laid."[40]

Part of LaVern's effectiveness as a leader was her ability to make judicious decisions and to motivate her associates to move the Primary program forward. Dwan J. Young, who was called to the Primary general board in 1970 and who later became the seventh general president of the Primary, observed about LaVern, "I have never seen anyone who could scan a paper, absorb what was there, make a decision, and present an assignment as she did. She was remarkable that way. I would just sit in awe of her ability to evaluate and then to make judgments. I came at the end of her career when she had had so much experience. I learned a lot from her. I just loved her dearly, but at first I was a little frightened of her. When she spoke, you listened. Yet she was a very kind woman."[41]

LaVern reorganized the general presidency so that each member was responsible for certain areas of the Primary program, repeating that pattern on the stake and ward levels. Since boys were her "specialty," she kept the boys' programs for the president. Counselors in the presidency supervised the other age groups, music, programs, activities, and in-service training for leaders. She also reduced the stake boards to seven members: the Primary presidency, secretary, music director, organist, and in-service leader. "This was our feeling that the presidency should supervise the teachers," stated LaVern. "When I met with the presidents of the stake in my conference, I would talk to them about their responsibilities. Then when the stake met with their ward presidents, . . . they would then give the ward presidents [the same] instructions."[42] Then the ward presidents would go back and give the instructions to their teachers.

This change had great impact on the Primary organization. Years later, Vickie Stewart, LaVern's granddaughter, commented, "Her standardization of the responsibilities of a Primary presidency was very helpful. Many people have told me that the Primary was on the cutting edge of doing things better—better manuals, better organization, and they appreciated that. She was an innovator and did things that nobody else had thought of before in the Church."[43]

Assessing the needs of Primary units throughout the ever-growing Church, the Primary presidency reorganized age groups and gave most classes new names. Zions' Boys and Girls became Co-Pilots and Top Pilots; the Junior Groups were given the names Sunbeams, Stars, and Rainbows, later changing to Moonbeams, Sunbeams, CTR Pilots and Right Way Pilots; the nine-, ten-, and eleven-year-old girls were no longer Larks, Bluebirds, and Seagulls, but Gaynotes, Firelights, and Merrihands, together known as Lihomas (Little Home Makers). The older boys were still known as Trail Builders (Blazers, Trekkers, and Guide Patrol.)[44]

One of the lasting contributions of LaVern's administration was the introduction of a new Primary song, "I Am a Child of God," at the April 1957 Primary conference. LaVern had asked Naomi W. Randall, a member of the general board, to write a song focusing on the importance of teaching children the gospel and suggested she collaborate with Mildred T. Pettit, who lived in Pasadena, California. Naomi wrote the words and then sent them to Mildred, who composed the music in one week. The song was published in the June 1957 *Children's Friend* and became an instant favorite.[45]

Recognizing the need to improve teaching, the Primary published two resources for teacher training: *Three Steps to Good Teaching* in 1960 and *The How Book* in 1968.[46] During that period, the Church introduced the correlation program, which not only correlated all materials used by the various auxiliaries but also placed all Church programs under the umbrella of priesthood supervision. For the Primary, as well as the Relief Society and YWMIA, this meant turning over manual preparation, teacher training, and financial management to Church correlation committees. LaVern said, "I think the correlation program was inspired by President Lee. I think it was a hard adjustment, but I agree that it's the right thing."[47]

LaVern traveled widely, visiting many areas of the world where there was a stake or mission organized, including Japan, Taiwan, Korea, Singapore, the Philippines, Okinawa, Africa, South America, New Zealand, and Australia. In 1966 she and Tom, who represented the Sunday School board, traveled together to Central and South America. She was also the first general auxiliary leader to visit East Germany. Saints in the Dresden area thrilled to hear her speak to them.

LaVern was loved by Primary children everywhere as well as by her co-workers. For her birthday in January 1966, children from her own ward visited her home, sang to her, and presented her with a cake. At the April 1966 Primary conference, a surprise tribute was given to her by her counselors, Leone W. Doxey and Lucile C. Reading, for her twenty-five years of Primary service.

"The First Lady of American Scouting"

LaVern was an enthusiastic Scouter. The Boy Scouts' announcement of a new policy in 1950 that lowered the age of entrance for boys into the Scouting program from twelve to eleven presented a difficult dilemma for the Church: Should eleven-year-old boys enter Young Men's Mutual Improvement Association to participate in Scouting, or should Scouting for eleven-year olds be included in Primary? Initially, in 1950, the Primary presidency recommended giving all responsibility for Scouting to the YMMIA and letting Primary focus on priesthood preparation. For a time that plan was followed, but it was filled with obstacles, especially in developing areas of the Church. Boys, expected to attend both Primary and Scout meetings each week, most often ended up going to only one. Finding available Scout leaders presented a problem, as did transportation for youth in wards whose membership was spread out over great distances.[48]

In May 1952, Scouting for eleven-year-old boys became part of the Primary program. In addition, Cub Scouting, which had been solely a community program, was also given to the Primary to oversee. LaVern felt overwhelmed by these new responsibilities in addition to supervising the *Children's Friend,* the Primary Children's Hospital, and all the other Primary programs. She remarked to Church President David O. McKay, "That's just like going up against a stone wall." He responded, "The wall may seem insurmountable but we cannot stand back and say there is no use trying. We can walk the distance to the wall. We are not discharging our duty until we go up to it, and when we do that there may be a hidden ladder which we have not seen, or over here there may be a door through which we can pass. Now if you come up against a wall, let me know. But we must hold to our ideals and teaching of the gospel. We cannot compromise on that."[49]

LaVern's brother Blaine Watts was chairman of the Scout committee on the YMMIA board during the early years of her administration. She remarked, "He knew Scouting and he was a great help to me. I conferred with him often and he could always answer my questions and give me the help I needed. He was a great strength to me and supported the Primary program wholeheartedly."[50]

The class for eleven-year-old boys, designated as the Guide Patrol, had a dual function in preparing boys to receive the priesthood as well as in advancing them in the Scouting program. The Primary published the *Guide Patrol Digest* in 1957 to fully explain the two programs. Whereas members of the Guide Patrol met with other members of the Primary on a weekday, Cub Scout den meetings were held on a day other than Primary and generally in a home. (Cub Scouting was under the direction of the Primary but not included as part of the Primary curriculum.)

Since Primary was a weekday program, men were generally not available to serve as Scout leaders in Primary. When Primary leaders petitioned the national Scout committee to allow women to serve, one leader assured Primary leaders that although women could serve, they would not be officially recognized. Within a few years, not only were women allowed to wear the Scout uniform and be fully registered, but in 1967 LaVern Parmley also became the first woman to serve on a national Scout committee—the National Religious Relationships Committee—and in 1976 was the first woman to receive the Silver Buffalo. She was also named a member at large of the National Council of Boy Scouts and a member of the Cub Scout Committee. As Primary general president, she served as a member of the General Scout Committee of the Church, attended national and international Boy Scout jamborees, and was a faculty member at the Philmont Scout Ranch in New Mexico.

The Great Salt Lake Council of the BSA, on whose executive board LaVern served, honored her with its first Silver Fawn award in 1971, printing in their program:

"As General President of the Primary Association of the Church of Jesus Christ of Latter-day Saints for the past twenty years, LaVern W. Parmley has been a veritable crusader in the interest of wholesome activity and spiritual development for young people. Local, regional, and national Scouters often refer to her as the 'first lady of American Scouting,' she having served with distinction on the National Cub Scout and Religious Relationships committees and as a Member at Large of the National Council, Boy Scouts of America. Probably no other woman has done more to develop and conserve America's most precious resource—Boypower—a most worthy nominee for the first Silver Fawn Award in the Great Salt Lake Council."[51]

The New Hospital

LaVern had been a counselor in the general presidency during the initial phases of the construction of the new Primary Children's Hospital, located at Twelfth Avenue and D Street in Salt Lake City. As president, she assumed responsibility for supervising the facility's completion and for its

funding and operation. On February 12, 1952, the day scheduled to move young patients from the old Hyde home to the
new facility, one of the worst blizzards of the winter struck the
city. Since all the medications, equipment, and supplies had
been moved the night before to the new hospital, LaVern had
no choice that day but to follow the original plan.
Ambulances, buses, and "every available means" carried the
children from the Hyde home in downtown Salt Lake City up
the steep hill to their new residence.

President David O. McKay dedicated the new building,
which had been under construction for three years, in March
1952. Primary Children's Hospital was no longer a convalescent hospital but a full-service, up-to-date children's hospital
with facilities for surgery, radiology, laboratory work, speech
and dental treatment, and adolescent care.

Though LaVern was a great administrator and leader with
vision, she also thought of little details to make the children's
stay in the hospital more pleasant. She asked a seamstress to
make hospital gowns of brightly colored materials so that children could choose what they wanted to wear each morning
and not have to wear the same drab gowns every day.
Occasionally, she asked the Primary general board members
to fast for a particular patient. She also worked with priesthood
leaders in providing sacrament services in the hospital for
patients to attend each Sunday.

By 1964, a little over a decade after its dedication, the
hospital had outgrown the original building and needed to be
enlarged. To help pay for a new wing, LaVern asked each of
Primary's 75,000 officers and teachers throughout the Church
to earn a dollar to donate and to report how they earned it.
Their combined efforts far exceeded the $75,000 goal, produc-
ing $103,000. Some leaders sold pine nuts, did janitorial work,
packed and sorted apples, cut lawns, gave luncheons, baked
pumpkin pies, sold rides on donkeys, trimmed poodles, made
floral arrangements, and washed cars. One woman who had
several young children said she had too much to do, so she
paid herself a dollar to just sit down and rest.[52] Construction
on the new wing, which doubled the number of beds in the

hospital, was completed in June 1966. Several years later, because of the expanded services of the hospital, LaVern suggested that it be renamed the Primary Children's Medical Center.

LaVern, as chairman of the board of trustees and as one who had spent considerable time with the children, was understandably pleased with the hospital. In an interview preserved as an oral history and conducted after her release as Primary general president, she explained, "I think the most rewarding thing I've ever done in my life is to work with the hospital and to see what the hospital has been able to accomplish and how many children it has helped."[53]

As a prelude to other major organizational changes that would take place over the next several years, LaVern was appointed vice-president of the board of trustees of the hospital in 1970, when Bishop Robert L. Simpson, of the Presiding Bishopric, became chairman. In 1974 the Church divested itself of all hospitals.[54] For LaVern, that was a sad day.

"When they took away the hospital, . . . that about broke my heart," she recalled. "I was there when they built this whole big new hospital, raised the money, and helped to work all the plans, and moved the children from the old hospital to the new hospital. It was just part of my life and I knew all those children and I've seen many of them out in the countries when I've visited there and they were well and happy. That was just the pinnacle of love. I don't think anything will ever be as tremendous as a Primary Children's Hospital when I see what that has done for children from all over the world."

LaVern admitted, however, that the hospital "was a tremendous responsibility. I often say that whenever I meet Sister [Louie B.] Felt and Sister [May] Anderson—they were the ones that had the idea of that hospital for children and they called it a dream they had—I'm going to say, 'It was easier to have the dream than it was to run the hospital.'"[55] Bronze plaques were placed at both entrances of the board room honoring LaVern for her years of service to the hospital.

Fortunately, the Primary Children's Medical Center, though now administered by a nonprofit health care corporation, has not only continued in operation but has moved to new, larger facilities near the University of Utah Medical Complex. The center is now one of the foremost children's hospitals in the nation.[56]

"Send a Friend *on a Mission"*

As Primary president, LaVern also served as the editor of the *Children's Friend*. Although the day-to-day publication work was handled by a staff drawn from the general board and professional writers and artists, LaVern was very involved in the production of the magazine. "I was responsible for anything that went in the magazine," she said. "I had to make final decisions. We did all the editing; we read all the proof."[57] During the 1950s, the Primary sponsored publication of two story books, *The Children's Friend Storybook for Younger Children* and *The Children's Friend Storybook for Older Children*. The Primary also started a campaign to send "a *Friend* on a mission," asking children to donate nickels and dimes to buy subscriptions to send the magazine to mission areas. According to LaVern, that program "was very, very successful. We had many, many stories come to us of families that were brought into the Church because of the magazine."[58]

In 1970, responsibility for publishing the *Children's Friend* was shifted from the Primary to the Church Publications Committee as part of the effort to correlate all the Church's official printed and instructional materials. Lucile C. Reading, a former member of LaVern's presidency, was named managing editor of the magazine, which was renamed the *Friend* in 1971.

Blessings and Support

LaVern enjoyed two blessings that helped her greatly in her service as Primary president. One was a very supportive husband and the other was unusually good health. Her sister June Watts Jensen said, "Her support at home enabled her to be available to do all that she did. I've never seen a man support a wife as Tom did while LaVern was in the Primary."[59]

Nick Watts added, "Even though Tom was a man of great distinction and honor, he never would try to outdo LaVern. He always placed himself in the background and in a position of support, and he felt his mission was to help her do her calling."[60] Once when LaVern was traveling for the Primary, a friend brought a bushel of grapes to the Parmley home. Tom, seeing the need, washed, steamed, and juiced the grapes so that LaVern could make grape jelly when she returned.[61] LaVern said of her husband, "Tom has given me his full support in this position. I never heard one word of complaint. He always said, 'This is your job. That is that you have been called to do. You go. Don't worry about me. I'll be all right.' All the time I traveled, at every stop there was always a letter waiting for me [from Tom]."[62]

"In the 27 years I've been on the board," LaVern stated, "I've never missed an assignment because of ill health. . . . I have been promised that I would have my health in carrying out my responsibilities."[63] Once, however, LaVern required surgery, which was performed on the Saturday prior to an April conference. She was released from the hospital on the following Tuesday. Her doctor gave her permission to attend Primary general conference two days later on the condition that she spend several days resting in bed afterwards. "When I got down to the Tabernacle Thursday morning, President [Harold B.] Lee was there and he'd brought Elder Sterling W. Sill and he said, 'I want to give you a blessing LaVern, before you go into your conference.' And he blessed me that it would be a conference such as I had never experienced and that I would have angels attend me. And truly I did. I could feel it. I conducted all the meetings and I stood in line and shook hands with two thousand Primary workers and I didn't have to go home and go to bed afterwards."[64]

She was an "incredible administrator," according to her granddaughter Vickie Stewart. "One time I asked her how she got everything done. She said, 'I get up every morning and I do what there is to be done. Then I go to bed at night. The next day I do it again.' I learned from her that it's the willingness to do the day-to-day labor that eventually results in big things."[65] Trilba Lindsay noted, "LaVern was a very careful and very strong leader, but she also delegated. She had a lot of trust for her board members. The Primary was a close-knit and a well-knit organization."[66] "Mother was an executive, who was focused, goal-driven, and accomplished a lot," said Frannie. "She knew what it took to make something happen. She could figure out where she was, where she wanted to be, and how to get there. That was her greatest strength. She spent little time or energy worrying about inconsequential things."[67]

Trail Builder

During her more than twenty-three years of service as Primary general president, LaVern received numerous honors and awards from the Church, Scouting, and the community, including Honorary Golden Gleaner (1965); Outstanding Citizen Award, Boy Scouts of America (1969); Woman of the Year, International Sertoma Club (1970); Utah State Medical Association Annual Award of Merit (1971); Silver Fawn (1971); election to the Salt Lake Council Hall of Fame (1973); Minuteman Award, Utah National Guard (1973); Distinguished Service Award, Salt Lake County Medical Society (1974); Merit Honor Award, University of Utah Emeritus Club (1975); Exemplary Woman of the Year, Ricks College (1975); and Scouting's impressive Silver Buffalo Award (1976).

She served on the Utah Governor's Committee for Children and Youth; served two terms as a trustee of the National Association of Children's Hospitals and Related Institutions; served three terms as president of the Utah Lung Association; was on the boards of the Traveler's Aid, Utah Tuberculosis and Health Association, and Deseret Gymnasium; and was a member of the Women's Legislative Council.

LaVern was released as general president of the Primary on October 5, 1974, at general conference. She then taught mother education lessons in her ward Relief Society and enrolled in an institute class. She took needlepoint classes and was frequently invited to give speeches and book reviews. She commented, "I have not regretted my release at all. I have found so many interesting things to do. I have felt that I did the best I could while I was in the Primary in the 23 years I was in the presidency and . . . [the] ten years [I was] a counselor."[68]

LaVern Watts Parmley died of a heart attack on January 27, 1980, in a Salt Lake hospital at age eighty. Following funeral services held in the Hillside Stake Center, she was buried in the Salt Lake City Cemetery, just a few blocks from Primary Children's Medical Center, where she had served so faithfully.

During the thirty-three years she served in Primary as a general board member, counselor, and general president, LaVern was a trail builder. She developed the boys' program, her "specialty," integrated the Cub Scout and the Blazer Scout programs in Primary, reorganized the age groups and classes, standardized responsibilities of Primary presidencies, stream-lined stake boards, oversaw the completion and then expansion of Primary Children's Hospital, and published storybooks for children, in addition to improving the quality of the *Children's Friend*. She sought to better the lives of the children over whom she presided, her motivation being, according to her husband, that "she loved the gospel; she loved Primary; she loved everybody."[69] Frannie said, "Mother cared desperately about the welfare of children. That's what she wanted to change and to have some say about. She truly had great impact on the lives of children."[70]

6

Naomi Maxfield Shumway
1974–1980

I often liken Naomi Shumway to the Naomi in the Bible because she is so wise," said Dorthea C. Murdock, who served as a counselor in the Primary general presidency. "As president, she had an ability to sort things out, to organize, and to look ahead and discern what would be good for children. Her focus was on children. When she prayed, you were moved because you knew she was so touched with the spirit and purpose of Primary and what Primary meant to children and families. You felt her love for every child, everywhere, no matter where or what their circumstances. You knew that she was close to the Lord in her calling and responsibility to take care of children."[1]

A keen interest in and love for children, a zest for organization, and a deep spirituality characterize Naomi Maxfield Shumway, the sixth general president of the Primary.

Family Roots

The Maxfield family's roots go back to Cheshire County in northern England, and the family was established in that locale prior to William the Conqueror's invasion in 1066. Centuries later, in 1818, Naomi Maxfield Shumway's paternal great-great-great-grandparents, John and Hannah Appleton Maxfield, and their children sailed from England with the intent of immigrating to Australia. But when their ship wrecked at sea, a passing freighter rescued the passengers and took them to Nova Scotia, Canada. The Maxfields prospered on Prince Edward Island, where they settled. John Ellison Maxfield, Naomi's great-great-grandfather, married Sarah Elizabeth Baker, who had also immigrated to Canada from England.

Two missionaries of The Church of Jesus Christ of Latter-day Saints visited Prince Edward Island in 1844 and preached the gospel at a meeting John Ellison Maxfield attended. Family tradition reports that when he returned home from the meeting, he gathered his family together and said, "I have just heard what I have been looking for all my life."[2] He was baptized in October of that year.

John and his family left Prince Edward Island in 1850 to join the Saints in the Salt Lake Valley. They sacrificed much in going to Zion.

In Salt Lake, John and his sons established sawmills and mines and helped build the first road into Big Cottonwood Canyon. John and Elizabeth's second son, Richard, who was Naomi's great-grandfather, became so adept at measuring wood that he could calculate the footage of a wagonload of lumber by merely looking at it. Brigham Young requested that he select the lumber for the Salt Lake Tabernacle.

Naomi's paternal great-grandmother, Artemissa Ann Harris, whom Richard Maxfield married in Salt Lake City in 1854, was born in Carrollton, Illinois, in 1835 and made the trek to Salt Lake City in 1848.

After their marriage in 1854, Artemissa and Richard Maxfield lived on a farm in South Cottonwood and became parents of eight children, including William Albert Maxfield, Naomi's grandfather. Richard served two missions and helped haul granite from Little Cottonwood Canyon for the Salt Lake Temple.

Naomi's grandmother, Johanna Olsen, whom William Albert Maxfield married, emigrated with her parents from Norway because her father's foreman gave him the ultimatum of leaving the Church or losing his job. The Olsens settled in

Provo, where Johanna and William met. After their marriage in 1893, they bought a farm in Vineyard, a few miles north of Provo, where their oldest son and Naomi's father, Albert Elias Maxfield, was born.

On her mother's side, Naomi's roots also go back to England. Elizabeth Short, Naomi's great-grandmother, was born in London, England, in 1841. She moved to South Africa in 1850 with her parents. Five years later the family joined the Church. Along with her mother, brothers, and sister, she sailed from the Cape of Good Hope in 1863, arriving in Utah six months later. The following year she married Philander Brown, a farmer, carpenter, and railroad foreman. Philander, who was born in Rush, New York, had joined the Church in 1859 and was living in Salt Lake City when he met Elizabeth. Their son William married Henrietta Clinger in 1895. The woman who would become Naomi's mother—Orilla May Brown, daughter of William and Henrietta—married Albert Elias Maxfield in 1914. Seven years later, in 1921, they were sealed in the Salt Lake Temple.

"Determined to Succeed"

Naomi Maxfield was born October 3, 1922, in Provo, Utah, the fourth of Albert and Orilla's six children. Naomi has an older sister, Leah, two older brothers, Albert Vard and Wendell Dean, and a younger brother and sister, Ronald Grant and Karen.

Naomi's father, Albert, was an upholsterer by trade. She remembers him as being "very artistic with his hands and very capable. All six of us children had furniture that my father had either reupholstered or built from scratch."[3] Her mother, a skilled seamstress, served for many years as homemaking leader in Relief Society. According to Naomi, "The Depression years were hard years, and we struggled financially. The statement, 'We weren't poor; we just didn't have any money,' described our family's situation. But Mother was very creative and a great homemaker. We were a close family and enjoyed family gatherings."[4] One of Naomi's early memories is of going to the Fourth of July Parade in Provo each year. She recalled her mother making holidays memorable for the family.

Naomi's sister Leah, who is six years older than Naomi, commented, "Naomi was a darling little girl. She was very determined to succeed in the things that she planned, even when she was small. She was a good student. She also had a lot of friends."[5] Those two traits, determination and the ability to develop close friendships, have been evident throughout Naomi's life.

When Naomi was five years old, the Maxfields moved from Provo to Salt Lake City, where they lived in the LeGrand Ward in the central part of the city. Naomi enjoyed her growing-up years in her neighborhood and ward. She remembers going to Primary as a child, reciting the Articles of Faith to her teacher, and participating in a number of programs. She remembers experiencing a "good feeling" at Primary.[6] In that ward was a group of girls the same age who attended the same schools, participated together in Primary and YWMIA classes and activities, and, as a result, became lifelong friends. Some grew especially close while they were Gleaners in the YWMIA program. For fifty years, they have met together monthly with their teacher, Jean Latter. Their summer and Christmas parties have included their husbands. Naomi commented, "The friendships you make as a young girl you cherish, and your friends influence your life by their way of life and their standards. I don't remember now the specific lessons we had, but I remember the sisterhood of those choice friends. I think the gospel just kept us having that in common and kept us together."[7]

Orilla, Naomi's mother, taught in the Primary and Relief Society, but Albert, her father, was not active in the Church during her growing-up years. "Mother always encouraged us in our Church activities," Naomi said, "and she not only told us to respect our father, but she also set an example in doing so."[8] After some of the Maxfield children were married, Albert became reactivated and served a stake mission.

Naomi attended Roosevelt Junior High and East High School. After graduation, she went to work in an office at Hill

Air Force Base, north of Salt Lake City. There she met a young airman, Rod Shumway, who had been attending Utah State University in Logan before he went into the service. "He was a fun person, and our friendship grew over the years," said Naomi.[9] Rod thought Naomi stood out among the other office workers because "she dressed nicely and was quiet, refined and hardworking."[10]

Marriage, Family, and Miracles

Naomi and Roden Grant Shumway were married in the Salt Lake Temple on March 8, 1945, while he was home on leave from the Air Force. Naomi accompanied him back to his base in Los Angeles but stayed only for a short while because she needed to return to work at Hill Field. Fortunately, Rod was again transferred to Hill Field and stayed there until he was released from active duty. He continued to serve for more than twenty years as a reserve officer.

Rod went into the banking business, and the Shumways made their home in Salt Lake City. He then had an opportunity to open Pioneer Savings and Loan in Bountiful, and the family moved to that community, just north of Salt Lake City, in 1963. Several years later, Rod became president of State Savings and Loan.

The Shumways' first child, Sharene (Shari), arrived in March 1949, followed by Jana Lee (Jan) and Roger Grant within the next six years. The family found their Salt Lake and Bountiful neighborhoods and wards like an extension of family, and Naomi was grateful for the children's "good friends and schools."

Health crises with their children helped Naomi and Rod grow in faith and reliance upon the Lord. Jan became ill with rheumatic fever when she was in kindergarten. Sustained by the faith and prayers of her family, she recovered. Then Roger, at age eight, was diagnosed as having a tumor, and the prognosis was not good. His family sought the Lord's help through their prayers and through priesthood blessings administered to him. The night before Roger was scheduled for surgery, Rod gave him a blessing. When the doctors operated on him the next day, they found only a pseudo-tumor—a miracle in the Shumways' eyes. "Roger lived and fulfilled all the blessings we could have ever hoped for him," Naomi said.[11]

As Jan was growing up, she learned from her mother that organization was a supreme virtue. She also learned other lessons from her. Jan said, "Mom is quiet and loving. She knows what is right. She could always instill in us the desire to do our best. She could talk to you and get you to see different aspects of a situation and then make you feel like it was your idea. She has a gentle, happy sense of humor. She has a wonderful spirit about her. I loved to listen to her pray. It always made me feel as if Heavenly Father was right there."[12]

"Mom and Dad were so supportive," said Roger. "If they couldn't be there physically, we still knew they were supporting us. For example, when I graduated from college, they were on their way to East Germany on a Church assignment, so they called me from London to congratulate me."[13]

Family Traditions

"Naomi really likes traditions," observed Dorthea Murdock.[14] Partly due to traditions instilled by her parents and partly as a result of her own enthusiasm, she has carried on meaningful traditions throughout her life.

For generations, Christmas has been the favorite holiday of Naomi's family. The Maxfield clan gathered at Naomi's parents' home for Christmas breakfast for years, but when the family numbered sixty or seventy members, they had to find a larger place—usually a church meetinghouse.[15] Jan recalled that when she was a child, "on Christmas morning, soon after we had enjoyed opening our presents, we got up and went over to my grandparents' home. The Maxfield family would always dress up for special occasions. Gifts were exchanged with cousins. I cherish those times we spent with my aunts, uncles, and cousins. My grandparents set some strong family traditions that will be carried on from generation to generation."[16]

The Maxfield tradition became the Shumway tradition. All

of Naomi and Rod's family gather at their home for Christmas Day brunch, for which Naomi bakes her Christmas sausage and egg casserole. Another of her Christmas traditions is her cookie tree from which the grandchildren and other guests can choose their favorite cookies.

Other holidays and birthdays also have been festive occasions at the Shumway home. Shari remembered her mother making "a big deal out of birthdays with special cakes and fun parties."[17] Easter, with its traditional egg hunt for the grandchildren, and parades of all kinds at all seasons have been parts of the Shumway traditions.

From the time Naomi attended the Fourth of July parades in Provo when she was a young girl, she has loved parades. The Shumways still go to the Provo parade each year. The night before Bountiful's July 24 parade, she and Rod set up lawn chairs along the parade route in Bountiful so that the family can see the parade together. Part of the fun includes the bag of treats that she brings.

The Shumways enjoyed taking trips together to Disneyland in southern California and to Yellowstone National Park in Wyoming, though Naomi claims that they were not a "camping family." Some trips included a parade, such as the Rose Bowl Parade in Pasadena, California. Getting together with their extended families has been a highlight for Naomi, Rod, and their children. Rod grew up in Kanab, in southern Utah, where his parents raised cattle on land they owned outside of town. Every Memorial Day the entire Shumway family goes to Kanab for a reunion. "That is very important to our grandchildren. It helps them to know their heritage and to keep them close to their family," said Naomi. "We also enjoy the Maxfield family reunions. Once a year the adults, around fifty of us, get together for an evening of food and entertainment. In the summer, we have a reunion for everyone, which numbers about two hundred."[18]

Often members of the Shumway family, including the children, their spouses, and the twelve grandchildren, have dinner together at Rod and Naomi's home. According to Jan, her mother is "a fabulous cook and makes everything from scratch. It is almost therapeutic for her. She makes wonderful meals and sets a beautiful table."[19] Some of the family's favorite dishes are her homemade rolls, baked beans, potato salad, cheesy potatoes, salsa and cream cheese with chips, sweet pickles, and chili sauce.

Reaping the Rewards of Church Service

"All her life Naomi has been a teacher," commented her sister Leah.[20] Her first opportunity to teach Primary came after she graduated from high school. Naomi then worked in the Junior Sunday School in the LeGrand Ward. After she was married and living in another ward, she served as a counselor in the YWMIA presidency and as a teacher in Junior Sunday School. From the time she taught Primary again when Roger, her third child, was a baby until the time she was released as general president of the Primary in 1980, she served continuously in Primary. All of her experiences involved teaching—whether in the classroom with children or as a leader instructing other adults. She served as a ward and then a stake Primary president. Recalling his mother's service in Primary, Roger drew from this experience and helped organize home Primaries in Paris, France, while he was serving as a missionary. As adults, Naomi's daughters Shari and Jan have both served in ward and stake Primary leadership positions as well.

In 1963 the Shumways moved into their new home in Bountiful, a few days before school started. Naomi enrolled the children in school and started unpacking boxes. The first time the phone rang after it was connected, LaVern W. Parmley, the Primary general president, asked Naomi to come to her office for an interview. LaVern extended to Naomi a call to serve on the general board of the Primary with an assignment on the In-service and Trail Builder committees. She later became chairman of the in-service, stake conference, and Trail Builder committees. As chairman of the Blazer committee, she supervised developing new lessons and programs for ten- and eleven-year-old boys. Another challenging assignment was introducing the new programs and manuals at the annual

Primary general conference. When Naomi began her service on the general board, all board members were involved in writing lessons—"before the days of computers or xerox machines," Naomi recalled. "We also did all the proofreading and overseeing of the printing."[21]

When Naomi was set apart as a member of the general board, she was told in the blessing given to her by Elder William J. Critchlow, "The things that you will have to postpone to accept this calling are inconsequential to the blessings you will receive." Throughout the years she served on the board, she felt that she was blessed many times over.[22]

The Shumway children found that their mother's service added a new dimension to their lives. Jan said, "Mom was called to the general board when I was twelve. I started thinking about the Church worldwide instead of just in Bountiful. It was a wonderful time for us because of the spirit she had, her love of children, and the stories she would tell us about her travels. I didn't feel that Primary interfered with our lives. Mom arranged her Primary work around our schedules and was there at all of our functions. She never made a big deal of anything; she never bragged. She could be up all night long, but we didn't know that."[23]

Because she still had children at home, Naomi most often visited stake conferences in Utah, which entailed training meetings on Saturdays and two sessions of stake conference on Sundays.

Sixth General President

In 1973, Naomi accompanied LaVern W. Parmley to a Scout jamboree. While at the camp, Naomi started hemorrhaging. Bishop Vaughn J. Featherstone of the Presiding Bishopric gave her a blessing, and after Naomi was examined by a doctor at camp, she flew home for surgery. When someone suggested that LaVern Parmley might be released soon, Naomi heard a voice say to her, "We'll wait for you." She dismissed that thought, but less than a year later, she received a telephone call inviting Rod and her to meet with President Spencer W. Kimball.

When they met with President Kimball, he asked Naomi to serve as the Primary general president and told her she was responsible for all the children in the world. He also told her that her presidency would not be for a lengthy time as several of her predecessors had experienced. She vowed to "work hard and really dedicate those years."[24]

On October 5, 1974, Naomi was sustained at general conference as the sixth Primary general president. Also sustained were her counselors, Sara Broadbent Paulsen and Colleen Bushman Lemmon. (Dorthea Christensen Murdock became second counselor when Sara was released in 1977 to serve as matron of the São Paulo Brazil Temple, and Colleen became first counselor.) Subsequently, thirty board members were called, some of whom, like Naomi, had served with LaVern W. Parmley. At the time of Naomi's calling, a half million children were enrolled in Primary.

When she returned home from general conference that afternoon she found a fragrant welcome; her neighbors, in a thoughtful gesture of support, had decorated her front porch with flowers. That night Naomi's bishop came to her house and told her that earlier he had received an impression of her new calling. Since her three children had left home that same year, with Shari moving to California, Jan getting married, and Roger serving a mission, she could freely devote her time and energy to Primary.

Rod helped Naomi in a variety of ways, from cooking his own dinner to keeping her car clean, filled with gas, and equipped with snow tires when the season dictated. He even made it his job to provide popcorn and soda pop for her to snack on when she stayed up late reading lesson manuals. Roger remembers his father literally rolling out a red carpet for Naomi when she returned from a traveling assignment. Jan observed that her parents worked well together and that Rod coached Naomi on how to manage an office because this was new to her.

Rod occasionally traveled with Naomi on assignments, and as he watched her conduct meetings, speak, and interact with other Primary leaders, he observed, "She recognized and had great respect for the priesthood. Her prayers reflected her strong testimony. She went about her work in a quiet manner. She is a person of diligence and dedication to the Lord."[25]

Administration

Not long after Naomi became president, a newspaper editor asked her what she was going to change in Primary. She replied, "I don't think I am going to change anything until I find out there is a reason to change."[26]

The theme throughout her administration was to "catch the vision of Primary." She instructed her board members that Primary is to "train, not entertain" and that any innovation should be measured "against the standard of spiritually strengthening every child."[27]

"Naomi is an organized and detailed person," stated Sara B. Paulsen, a counselor to Naomi. "If she had anything to do with a program or presentation, it had to be quality. She worked hard and expected others to do so as well. Her concern for children was basic in everything that was prepared, in everything that was done. How would it affect the children was uppermost in her mind. She was very much concerned that the Primary program be a worldwide program—not just something that would be effective here at Church headquarters, but that it would reach children in Germany or Brazil, for instance. She also wanted feedback from leaders in various areas to know if what we were giving them was effective in their circumstances."[28]

Trilba Lindsay, who served on the general board with Naomi and as the general secretary of the Primary, felt the key to Naomi's administration was her preparation. She said Naomi carried out her responsibilities with a lot of expertise. A perfectionist and dedicated leader, she expected others to faithfully fulfill their assignments in the same way. But because of her experience on the general board and knowing what it was like to be a committee member and a committee chairman, she would not give an assignment that she wasn't willing to do herself. She was very thoughtful, generous, and concerned about others.[29]

Dwan J. Young, who served on Naomi's board and who became the seventh Primary general president, noted: "Naomi is a quiet, refined, and dignified lady. She was very committed to the work and turned her whole life over to the Lord. We had a wonderful relationship as we traveled together and went to Philmont [a Scout training camp in New Mexico] every summer and the Scouting jamborees. She was a great teacher. She was very sensitive, but not demonstrative."[30]

Naomi's organization and desire for excellence were reflected in her diligence at carrying out her assignment. According to Dorthea Murdock, Naomi typically arrived early for a meeting and was extremely well prepared. "She was gentle and soft-spoken," commented Colleen Lemmon, "but firm when she felt strongly about something."[31]

At the last Primary general conference, which was held in April 1975, President Kimball announced that the auxiliaries would no longer hold such conferences because of the expense and travel difficulties involved. Rather, the Church "would take the program to the people"[32] through regional conferences. The general auxiliary presidencies—Primary, Relief Society, and Young Women—began to travel more extensively throughout the world. As Naomi visited Primaries in stakes and mission areas, she observed "a great sisterhood" among the faithful and dedicated Primary workers.

This period was also a time of transition and, as Sara B. Paulsen stated, a time to "enlarge our vision. We no longer sent out everything the leaders were to do. At first, it was a real concern for some leaders, but with experience they became more self-reliant and more reliant on the Spirit as they worked with the general guidelines from the Primary general offices."[33]

A Hundred Years of Primary

The Primary general presidency joined nine thousand Primary children on July 15, 1978, in the Children's Parade in downtown Salt Lake City to celebrate the one hundredth anniversary of the Primary Association. More than ninety stakes from surrounding areas created floats depicting various segments of Primary's history, activities, songs, and classes. For Naomi, who has loved parades all her life, participating in the centennial parade was a merging of her past joyful childhood memories with her hopeful dreams for the future of all Primary children.

From its small beginnings in 1878 when 215 children attended the first Primary meeting held in Farmington, Utah, the Primary, by its centennial, had grown to a worldwide organization of 540,000 children.

The Primary commissioned a play based on the life of Aurelia Spencer Rogers, who organized the first Primary. The musical, *Aurelia,* was presented at Promised Valley Playhouse in March 1978, with General Authorities and some of Aurelia's descendants as guests for opening night. An adapted version of the play was performed at the rock chapel in Farmington where Primary began. Wards and stakes throughout the Church put on this play as part of their year-long festivities.

A Primary plate, commemorating the celebration, was produced and sold. Two events concluded the centennial celebrations: local Primaries hosted fairs, much like the ones put on by Primaries in the nineteenth century; and the general presidency hosted a birthday dinner on August 11 in Salt Lake City. President Kimball and his wife, Camilla, were honored guests, along with other General Authorities and general auxiliary leaders and their spouses. Five hundred children presented "Primary on Parade," a review of Primary's one-hundred-year history.

Naomi summed up the purpose of the centennial: "The celebrations have been a time of reflecting upon the past, pondering upon the present, and committing to the future all in behalf of children."[34] She also said, "We are proud of the rich Primary heritage and the firm foundation that has been built these past 100 years. Our challenge as we begin the second century of Primary is to build that foundation even stronger and to ensure that the teachings of Primary are meaningful in the life of every child. The teachings of Primary must be strong, and the leadership effective as millions will be influenced by Primary in the future, not just thousands as in the past."[35]

Consolidated Meeting Schedule

As auxiliary leaders and General Authorities visited Church units throughout the world, they observed a need to simplify and consolidate some of the Church's programs. Among the factors contributing to this need were mounting fuel costs, distances that many members had to travel to meetinghouses, and the rise in the number of working women. A major challenge for Primary workers, Naomi observed, resulted from transportation difficulties. In urban areas, weekday Primary meetings often ended as rush-hour freeway traffic began, resulting in dangerous travel conditions. Many members could not afford the time or money to travel to meetings several times a week. For example, in the Philippines, Naomi was asked by local leaders, "Could we not have Primary on Sunday?"

In late 1979, the First Presidency announced the consolidated meeting schedule, to be implemented March 1, 1980, in the United States and Canada. Members of wards and branches would attend meetings during a three-hour period on Sundays. All members would attend sacrament meeting for seventy minutes. For the remainder of the time, children under twelve would be together in Primary, eliminating the need for the Junior Sunday School organization, while all members over age twelve attended Sunday School classes and separate priesthood, Relief Society, and Young Women meetings.

The change required that Primary workers, children, and parents all make adjustments. Some leaders wondered how they could keep the attention of children for an hour and forty minutes, and others were concerned about not being able to attend Sunday School and Relief Society. For Naomi, the new consolidated meeting schedule for Primary was "a combination of the best of both Junior Sunday School and Primary. There was more time to teach the gospel and more emphasis on the scriptures. It was important that Primary be the children's organization of the Church."[36] New Primary manuals were prepared, emphasizing the study of the scriptures, and the Articles of Faith became part of the curriculum for each age group.

"Scouting was Naomi's specialty," said her counselor Colleen B. Lemmon, who also had served on the general board with her.[37] Naomi helped to develop the Cub Scout Faith in God award and to introduce a manual for Cub Scouting in Canada. Serving as a member of the National Cub Scout Committee and of the executive board of the Great Salt Lake Council of the Boy Scouts of America, she received the Silver Fawn and the Silver Antelope awards.

Release and New Challenges

After serving for five and a half years, Naomi was released as Primary general president at general conference on April 5, 1980. She then taught a class of Merrie Miss girls in Primary, taught Spiritual Living in Relief Society in her home ward, and typed patriarchal blessings for the patriarch in her stake. When Rod was called as president of the Bountiful Heights Stake six months after her release in October 1980, she said, "It was my turn to support him."[38]

Even during the period of time when Rod served as stake president, Naomi found ways to contribute to the community. In 1982, Naomi was elected to the Utah State Legislature for one term. Her campaign theme was "Children are our most precious resource," and as a legislator she worked to protect the interests of children through more adequate school funding and through reducing classroom sizes.

After Rod's retirement as president of State Savings and Loan in 1983, he and Naomi took several institute classes together and did extensive traveling. They have been able to spend more time with their children, grandchildren, and friends and have "just tried to enjoy life," according to Naomi. Her daughter-in-law, Janet, said, "She "works at keeping the family close."[39] Naomi calls each family almost daily, attends the grandchildren's soccer and basketball games and piano and dance recitals, takes the younger ones to every new Disney or children's movie, and loves to shop for the children. Her home is a place where the grandchildren like to be. After a sixteen-year-old grandson had tried out for the school basketball team, he and a friend dropped by Naomi's home for encouragement and the familiar greeting, "You look like you are hungry." Naomi's flair for cooking has been a means of drawing her family closer together.

Naomi has encouraged spiritual growth in her grandchildren. When President Ezra Taft Benson urged all members of the Church to read the Book of Mormon, she bought a children's version of it for her three children's families. She wrote a note challenging them to read the Book of Mormon together.

She has carried on many of the traditions for her grandchildren that she started when her own children were young. Roger said, "Mom is unbelievable at Christmas. The grandkids get excited months ahead and all check about October to see if she is getting excited—which, of course, she is. She has this crazy little yell that the children love to hear. Every year she cooks fantastic meals and has presents galore. She loves Christmas."[40]

One Christmas Naomi received a computer and began compiling her family history on it. She also enjoys gardening, and according to her daughter-in-law, Janet Shumway, "She's really become an expert gardener. Their backyard is a floral masterpiece. She planted numerous perennials and moved them around until they looked just right."[41]

"Mom doesn't stop. She doesn't want to slow down," commented her daughter Shari. "She's still involved with many groups and civic activities. She's a member of the Women's State Legislative Council and has been on the board of advisers for the Bountiful/Davis Art Center, the American Association of Women, and Lakeview Hospital in Bountiful."[42] General board members who served under Naomi still get together for socials. Each summer they have a party to which the husbands are also invited. She still meets with her Gleaner class, her cousins group, and various study groups.

Not long after Rod retired, he experienced some serious health problems. "It's been a challenge for him because he is such an active, outgoing person," stated Naomi. "As a result, we have withdrawn from some of our activities. You accept things and enjoy what you can. This is where my place is now, making things comfortable for him and enjoying each other."[43]

During Naomi Maxfield Shumway's five-and-a-half-year administration as Primary general president, she "really gave her whole heart and soul," said Trilba J. Lindsay.[44] Whatever Naomi's involvement in her life—immediate and extended family, childhood friends, traditions, the legislature, Scouting, or Church service—she has prepared diligently, organized carefully, and given generously of herself. Like the Primary centennial, her life has been a celebration.

7

Dwan Jacobsen Young

1980–1988

When Dwan Young, Primary general president, visited a Bolivian Primary, one little girl reported that her class did not have a teacher that particular day. Dwan offered to fill in, and with the help of a translator, she taught the Primary class of five girls.[1] Her traveling companion and counselor, Virginia B. Cannon, observed, "She is a natural with children. She felt that each one was so important." Wherever the Primary general presidency traveled together, Virginia saw firsthand how Dwan "always took time to speak with children and get down on their level and see how they felt."[2]

On another occasion, Dwan attended Primary in Freiberg, East Germany, which at the time was under Communist rule. After their car was searched thoroughly and after their somber drive through a depressed and tightly guarded area of the city, Dwan and other members of her party entered the home that served as the LDS meetinghouse. "The most dramatic difference in spirit enveloped me," Dwan recalled. "It was a spirit of love, freedom, and the Savior."[3] Tears filled her eyes as she listened to twenty children fervently singing Primary songs in German.

As the seventh Primary general president, Dwan Jacobsen Young had many opportunities to visit Primaries from the South Pacific to Central America to the Far East and northern Europe as well as those near Church headquarters. In every setting, her love of the gospel and her love of children radiated to those she visited. "Dwan's warmth and love came through in everything she did," said Virginia. "She had a love for the people and a love for the children. They, in turn, responded to her with love."[4] Dwan's infectious enthusiasm, boundless energy, genuine love for people, and faith in the Savior have shaped her life, her relationships, and her service in the Church.

Pioneer Ancestors

Dwan's maternal great-great-grandfather, Reuben Miller, moved from Pennsylvania, where he was born, to Illinois in 1836. There he joined the Church in January 1843. He married Dwan's great-great-grandmother, Orice Burnham, in December 1845. The second of his four wives and a schoolteacher, Orice was born in New York of English ancestry.

The Miller family arrived in the Salt Lake Valley in September 1849.[5] They settled in Mill Creek, in the southeast part of the valley. Charles Eugene Miller, their only son and Dwan's great-grandfather, married Christine Graham McAllister in 1874. Her parents, who had heard the missionaries' message in their native Renfrewshire, Scotland, joined the Church and immigrated to Utah in 1860, when Christine was four years old.

Christine and Charles homesteaded one hundred and sixty acres in Riverton, in the southwest portion of the Salt Lake Valley. He also fulfilled a mission to the southern states.

Mary Edith Miller, the oldest of Charles and Christine's nine children and Dwan's grandmother, married her sweetheart and former schoolteacher, Solomon Elias Smith, in 1900. They settled in Draper, where S. E., as Solomon was known, again taught school. Vauna, Dwan's mother, was the oldest of their seven children.

Dwan's maternal great-grandfather, Absalom Wamsley Smith, was baptized in 1845. Then he took his family to Utah in 1852. One of his five wives was Mary Ann Osborn, the mother of Solomon Elias Smith.

Dwan's paternal great-grandfather, Thomas Jacobsen, was born in Denmark, where he joined the Church. He and his wife, Anna Marie Larsen, could not afford passage for the entire family to immigrate to Zion, so they, like many other Saints, sent their older children first. Before his daughters could earn enough money to bring the rest of the family, Thomas died. Dwan's grandfather, Andrew, only twelve years old at the time, came alone, and several years later his widowed mother and the younger children finally arrived. When Andrew arrived in Salt Lake City, he found work stocking shelves and delivering groceries for a grocery store. In 1892, he married Miriam Pearl Farmer and bought the store. Out of respect for his former employer, a Mr. Alexander, Andrew and Miriam named their second son, Dwan's father, Alexander Clifton Jacobsen.

Vauna Smith and Clif Jacobsen graduated from the LDS High School and then the University of Utah together. During those years, they courted, fell in love, and married. After their graduation, Vauna taught history at a junior high school, and Clif applied his business education to improving the grocery store.

A Neighborhood Filled with Children

Dwan Louise Jacobsen, the second child of Alexander Clifton and Vauna Smith Jacobsen, was born in Salt Lake City May 31, 1931. Her only brother, Alan, was four years older than she. Dwan grew up in the home, located on Kensington Avenue between Seventh and Eighth East Streets, that her mother and father had built before they were married. A grocer for many years, Clif was also the bishop of their ward for thirteen years and a member of the high council and stake presidency. Vauna, a homemaker, often helped out at the store, and she served on the Primary general board for seventeen years.

"My childhood was very, very happy," recalled Dwan. "Our neighborhood was filled with children. That was a wonderful place to grow up. We used to set up a Monopoly game on the neighbor's covered porch. Those games would go for three days. We played 'Run, Sheepie, Run' and 'Kick the Can.' There were five of us girls the same age. The Dionne quintuplets had just been born in Canada, so the five of us each took a name of the quintuplets, and we pretended we were those girls."[6]

Because Clif worked six days a week in the grocery business, the Jacobsens couldn't take long vacations. Nevertheless, they enjoyed a lot of time together at their family cabin in Lamb's Canyon, east of Salt Lake City. "Mom, my brother, and I would go up for a month in the summer," recalled Dwan. "Dad would come up two or three times a week. My fondest memories of summer are at the cabin. We hiked and caught chipmunks in a box with a stick and a string—the old-fashioned way."[7] Her brother, Alan, remembers picking wildflowers near the cabin, playing games, jacks, hopscotch, and horseshoes. "Mother allowed us to have one hour in the daytime to listen to the serials on the radio," he recalled. "There was nothing to do but make our own fun. We read a lot, and Mother and my aunt told us stories."[8] In the winter, all four of the Jacobsens skied, Dwan starting at age five with thirty-six-inch skis. She remembered having to climb up Ecker Hill in Parleys Canyon before skiing down—because ski lifts had not yet been built.

"The first long trip we went on was to the Arches. I remember all of us singing 'Put Your Shoulder to the Wheel' as we drove. Every time I hear that song I remember those experiences in southern Utah," said Dwan. "We did go to the Northwest on an educational trip. We saw the mountains where trees were cut, then visited pulp mills to see how paper was made. We went to Seattle and Portland and then down the coast. The only other long trip we took was after my brother was released from the Eastern States Mission; we met him and toured Church history sites."[9]

During her growing-up years, Dwan worked on Saturdays in her father's grocery store, located on Third Avenue and K Street in Salt Lake City, at first stocking shelves and then checking at the cash register.

As she observed her parents' lives, Dwan felt they were "both extremely giving people, always thinking about others."[10] She recalled that the day before her father died at age eighty-three, "he was cutting the lawn of one neighbor and fixing the plumbing of another. All my life my parents have been examples of Christlike love."[11] Dwan had daily opportunities to watch her parents' love in action; her brother, Alan, had suffered brain damage at birth and, as a result, had motor and speech impairments. She especially remembers her mother's patience and devotion in helping Alan develop basic skills. Her mother spent weeks preparing Alan to pass the sacrament as a deacon, helping him learn to balance the trays and to know which areas of the chapel he should serve. From helping her brother with his disabilities, Dwan developed traits she has retained throughout her life—the ability to love others, feel compassion, and exercise forgiveness as she watched other children tease him when he himself, as she said, "did not hold grudges and lived above that."[12]

Making Music

Early in her life, Dwan began piano studies, her mother serving as her first teacher. Following in the footsteps of her father, who was a fine cellist, she also learned to play the cello. Vauna observed, "Everything Dwan did as a child she did well. When she practiced the piano, she worked hard at it."[13] Dwan's sixth grade teacher, Mr. Reed, introduced his students to Shakespeare and other dramatists by adapting *As You Like It* and *HMS Pinafore* for his class to present. Dwan accompanied *HMS Pinafore,* which she felt was "a great experience for a twelve-year-old."[14] In junior high school, she played the piano for a dance teacher, which gave her sight-reading practice. Later she taught piano lessons.

While a student at South High School, Dwan was invited to play a Liszt piano concerto with the University of Utah Symphony. She was both thrilled and nervous about the opportunity but confident she would do well because she had prepared thoroughly. However, as the conductor raised his baton to cue her, she lost her concentration when she looked at someone she knew in the audience. Again the conductor raised his baton, but again she could not play even the first measure. Finally, one of the orchestra members handed her the music. Humiliated, she finished the piece without having to turn a page; she *did* have it completely memorized. When the concert was over, Dwan, vowing to never touch the piano again, wanted to disappear and not face her family and friends. But from this experience she learned that life goes on and that life is more valuable than a piano performance. She was grateful that her parents and teachers had prepared her to succeed in other ways by teaching her the gospel and that her mother encouraged her to continue her piano playing.[15]

Dwan was a leader among her peers, a good student, a cheerleader, and one of the first girls from South High to attend Girls' State. She met Thomas Young Jr., her future husband, when she was a senior in high school. He played the trumpet in a big band at Saltair, a resort on the shore of the Great Salt Lake, and had played with the University of Utah Symphony when Dwan made her infamous debut. When he noticed Dwan at a dance at Saltair, he persuaded a friend to introduce him to her. "I couldn't get her out of my mind," he recalled.[16] They dated until he received a mission call to England. "One of our famous dates was to go out on sign patrol for his father's electric sign company," Dwan remembered. "We drove up and down the streets and made note of which signs had outages."[17]

Dwan wrote to Tom while he was on his mission, dated other young men, and worked in the music department at the University of Utah while she pursued a degree in music and elementary education. When Tom returned from England in the fall of 1950, they resumed dating and became engaged at Christmas. Dwan and Tom were married June 22, 1951, in the Salt Lake Temple.

After their marriage, they both continued studies at the University of Utah, with Tom working part-time at Young Electric Sign Company. Eventually Tom worked full-time at the company, taking over more responsibility and later becoming president. In 1952, Dwan received a bachelor's degree in elementary education with an emphasis on music. Six weeks after she graduated, the principal of Libby Edward Elementary School, where she had been student teaching, asked her to teach band and orchestra. She was elated because teaching positions in music were difficult to find. She spent the summer "cramming" on the clarinet, flute, violin, trumpet, and other instruments she did not know how to play.

When she started teaching in the fall, she told her principal she would not be teaching long because she wanted to have a baby soon. But she taught longer than she planned, as Michael did not arrive until two years later, in 1954. Over the next decade, the Youngs had four more children: Paul, Christine, Suzanne, and Jeffrey. Christine was named after Dwan's great-grandmother, Christine McAllister Miller.

Each of the children learned to play musical instruments, particularly the trumpet and piano. Tom and the three boys formed a trumpet quartet. "My mother spent many hours teaching me to play the piano," Michael remembered. "Although I was not a very dutiful student, I developed a life-long love for music because of her efforts."[18]

Dwan joined in all the family sports activities, including both snow and water skiing, tennis, and hiking. The Youngs built a cabin together at Bear Lake, a beautiful lake straddling the Idaho-Utah border. There they enjoyed waterskiing. "Even though Mom has been able to water ski on one ski for years, she is always nervous just before the boat pulls out for another ride," said Jeff. "When she gets up on one ski, as she does every time, you should see her face and hear her gleeful screams from the end of the rope. We enjoy that."[19]

Tom, a licensed pilot, convinced Dwan to take flying lessons. "I took a pinch-hitter course in flying," she said. "I have taken ground school and can do everything but a controlled crash landing. I can keep the plane in the air, but I'm not sure I could get it on the ground."[20]

Family members have been amazed by Dwan's boundless energy. "She tackles anything that confronts her," stated her daughter Suzanne. "She's so active she wears me out."[21]

Paul, her second son, said, "She is the hardest worker I know—in church work or anything else."[22] Her husband described her as "more than conscientious."[23]

Underlying the music, adventures, and fun have been the love and concern the Youngs have for each other. "When we were teenagers, the family rule was to go in and report after we came home at night," said Christine. "I remember sitting on my parents' bed many times and talking about my evening. Mom was always there to listen. I appreciated that she was home when I came home from school, too. Thursday was her general board day so she was really busy that day, but I don't remember her being away a lot. When we were grown, she did a lot more traveling."[24] Tom and Dwan have had a close, happy relationship, according to their son Paul. "They often went on trips alone together and spent time together. Their love for each other is very evident. We enjoyed doing a lot of things together as a family. I don't know how they did it, but they instilled in each of us a great feeling of self-worth."[25]

Years of Preparation

Dwan's Church callings gave her a wide experience in working with children and in various leadership positions. She served in Cub Scouts, in Young Women, and on a Relief Society stake board. She was called as ward Primary president and then as a counselor in the Monument Park Stake Primary presidency. "I would only be in a position for about a year and a half to two years," she said. "I would just start feeling that I knew what I was supposed to do, and then I would be called to something else. I kept saying to myself, 'I'd like to stay somewhere long enough that I felt I could really make a difference.' It was frustrating." Later, when she was called to the Primary general board, she realized that "there had been purpose in all my experiences in many different areas."[26]

During the summer of 1970, the Young family took an extended trip to visit Church historical sites, as Dwan had done as a teenager with her parents. When they returned, before she had even had a chance to open the mail, the phone rang and LaVern W. Parmley, the Primary general president, identified herself. "Don't you answer your mail?" LaVern inquired. "There's a letter in the mail for you, and we expected you to be to a meeting last week. You have been called to the general board of the Primary."[27]

Although Dwan expected to serve on the music committee, she was surprised to be put on the Cub Scout Committee. Because of this assignment, she worked directly with LaVern Parmley, who supervised the Scouting program. Although Dwan's mother had served on the general board for seventeen years and Dwan was well acquainted with LaVern, she said, "At first I was a little frightened of her. When she spoke, you listened. Yet she was a very kind woman."[28] Later, when Dwan occupied the same position as LaVern, that of Primary president, she realized how valuable was the training she had received from LaVern.

When LaVern was released as general president in 1974, her successor, Naomi M. Shumway, asked Dwan to continue serving on the general board. She again worked on the Cub Scout committee and was in charge of a Primary Christmas pageant held at the Tabernacle on Temple Square for several years. Serving under Naomi's leadership also helped prepare Dwan for what was ahead.

Serving as the Seventh Primary General President

Early in 1980, an experience in the temple gave Dwan some uneasiness. She later called her mother, who, Dwan says, "is an incredible, faithful woman," and told her of her feelings. Vauna suggested she reread her patriarchal blessing. Still, Dwan was surprised to be called out of a committee meeting and told that President Spencer W. Kimball wanted to see her and Tom. When they met with him, Dwan wondered if Tom would be called as a mission president. President Kimball talked to Tom first about his father, as they had known each other many years before. Then he turned to Dwan and said, "Sister Young, we would like to call you to be the general Primary president." Stunned, she could only reply, "It's such a huge responsibility!" President Kimball leaned back in his chair and said, "I have a big responsibility, too." He then talked to her about the children of the world. "He was very sweet," she remembered. "That was a once-in-a-lifetime experience."[29]

The same day in March that Dwan met with President Kimball, her first granddaughter was born. When Dwan visited the new mother, her daughter Christine, at the hospital later that day, she gave no hint that her life was going to change. "She didn't want to overshadow the special event in our lives, the birth of our first child," Christine remarked.[30]

Dwan was sustained as the seventh Primary general president on April 5, 1980, at general conference, and subsequently set apart by President Kimball. She chose as her counselors Virginia Beesley Cannon and Michaelene Packer Grassli. Fourteen women were called to the general board.

The new presidency was sustained at a historic time for Primary. Worldwide, 588,000 children were enrolled in Primary. Just a month before conference, the consolidated meeting schedule had been implemented for the United States and Canada, and two months later, it would be implemented throughout the Church. "Our biggest challenge," recalled Dwan, "was to prepare a curriculum for a Sunday Primary. We had very little time. That's another miracle because ten years before, in 1970, was the first time that the Primary and Junior Sunday School leaders had even talked together about curriculum. There is no doubt in my mind that the Lord directed that to happen knowing what would be coming so that we would be prepared."[31]

With Primary now held on Sunday, many more men began serving—as teachers, nursery leaders, music leaders, and in-service leaders. Members of bishoprics also were able to attend Primary meetings and to speak to the children on occasion.

A significant concern with the new schedule was that nonmember children and children from less-active members' homes who had attended weekday Primary with their friends would not attend on Sunday. Attendance of these children did drop, and the general presidency encouraged local Primary leaders and teachers to invite them to Primary. Dwan recalled, "One of our other struggles was helping Church members recognize how important it is to teach children. Some women said, 'I can't miss Relief Society.'"[32] But Dwan believed that teachers would find "great joy and satisfaction in teaching. . . . They find that as they teach basic gospel principles, they are enjoying great spiritual growth."[33]

The lengthened Primary meetings provided children more opportunities to learn, give talks, sing, and dramatize what they had been taught. Sharing Time, initiated as part of the seventy-minute Primary segment, allowed the various classes to give presentations. Dwan noted as she observed Sharing Time in many Primary units that "when children reteach what they've learned, it solidifies classroom teaching."[34]

Not long after the announcement of the block schedule, the Quorum of the Twelve Apostles approved advancing Primary girls to the Young Women program when they turned twelve rather than having them graduate together at the end of the year as a class, as had been the previous practice. Thus, each girl would graduate from Primary, as the boys do, at age twelve. Over the next two years, new manuals were written and a curriculum developed for the Merrie Miss and Blazer B classes, so that when the children turned twelve, they would remain in their Primary class but meet with the Young Women or deacons quorum during Sharing Time.

Dwan and her counselors established a close relationship with the presidencies of the Relief Society and Young Women, who previously had worked quite independently of each other. In 1984, these auxiliary offices moved into the Relief Society Building, which had undergone extensive remodeling. "Visitors will be able to see how one program builds on the others, working to strengthen all three," Dwan commented.[35]

A Caring Administrator

Dwan's energy, genuine interest in others, and love for children unified her presidency and general board and helped them to "catch the vision of Primary." First counselor Virginia B.

Cannon found Dwan "active, full of energy, and never content to sit quietly," but at the same time "very receptive to counsel and open to board members' ideas and suggestions." She also felt Dwan was "tuned into the board members' personal lives and what their hopes and feelings were. At least once a year, she interviewed individual board members and, at their request, more often than that. She made everyone feel important and good. She was exceptional in working with others."[36]

Second counselor Michaelene P. Grassli, who succeeded Dwan as the Primary general president, remembered Dwan as a "mover and a shaker" in contrast to her own "deliberative style." She said, "Our presidency was very harmonious. Although we are not alike in some ways, we thought alike in most things and work moved fast. Much of that was due to Dwan's ability to lead—to set the pace and to unify us."[37]

Dwan discovered that the most rewarding aspect of her calling was visiting Primaries on every continent. Through these experiences, she felt she gained great insight into the needs of children in diverse places. "It made a dramatic difference in my feeling about what is needed. There is always a struggle to balance between the needs of the organized, sophisticated units of the Church, where people have been in the Church for many years, and the needs of the units where people have little experience, background, and resources. In the Philippines, for example," she said, "I found that lessons suggesting children write certain things on paper were inappropriate because they do not have paper."[38] As she visited Primary units throughout the world, children were "magnetized to her," said her husband, Tom, who occasionally accompanied her.[39] Even though she often could not speak their language, the children could feel her genuine love for them.

"We came at a time of cutting back," Dwan said. "We had to make Primary materials very basic and simple and then allow choices so that the units could do what was best for them. It meant that the sophisticated units would have to use their own ingenuity instead of our providing for them. We had to make them more self-reliant and think more about the world. It was a new day."[40]

In August 1984, the First Presidency announced the formation of area presidencies made up of members of the First Quorum of the Seventy, who presided over thirteen geographic regions of the Church. Observing the need for more experienced leadership in the outlying areas of the Church, Dwan, working with Relief Society general president Barbara W. Winder and Young Women general president Ardeth G. Kapp, suggested that the wives of these General Authorities be called to serve as area general board representatives. As these women served in various areas throughout the world, not only was leadership and information more effectively provided to local auxiliary leaders; Dwan also felt that the general leaders received valuable feedback from the field. To assist new leaders and leaders in developing areas, the Primary presidency developed a filmstrip, *Come with Me to Primary,* which depicted how a Primary meeting should function. They also produced a videotape on how to plan a successful Sharing Time because, as Dwan said, "A word on a page isn't sufficient for them to get the vision."[41]

During the time she served as Primary general president, Dwan felt she learned and grew more than she ever had before. At the general women's meeting in 1985, she said, "My calling is to care not only for the children in our church, but for the children in all the world. This is a tremendous responsibility, and at first I could feel only the burden of it. But I seek for the Lord's help constantly. I pray for enough strength and insight to do the work I have been called to do."[42] Later, she said, "I have become more reliant upon the Lord than I have ever been in my life. I feel more of a responsibility to study the scriptures, to be in tune, and to put my life in order so that I will be worthy to receive the inspiration and guidance that I need."[43] She further testified, "My dependence on Father in Heaven has become most intense. As that has occurred, the answers to prayer have come. I have always had a strong testimony of prayer, but I've never had such direct, sometimes almost instantaneous answers."[44]

A difficult aspect of the calling for Dwan was speaking. She felt frustrated in finding time to prepare the numerous talks she needed to give and in trying to meet the needs of particular audiences. Her daughter Suzanne observed, "As my mother grew in her calling, it became easier for her to speak in front of large groups. She was usually nervous and worried about giving a talk, and more so when it was in the Tabernacle. But speaking became easier for her, although she still spent a lot of time in preparation. She never wanted to give the same talk twice; she always wanted to have new material, to say something different.

"She would often share with us some of her faith-promoting experiences. As she visited Primaries throughout the world and saw people in such humble circumstances, their faith built her faith and really affected her."[45]

Primary and the Family

Dwan's service as Primary president was a positive experience for her family because of their willingness to support her and because they were still her primary concern. Jeff, who was in high school at the time, said, "My mother is a very positive, energetic person. She was bent on taking care of the house in spite of her responsibilities downtown. There were very few days that she didn't have breakfast on the table for me. She went out of her way to make sure the family was cared for. Whenever we called the office, our calls went through to her, no matter what she was doing. It was family first."[46]

Throughout his life, Paul has watched both of his parents tackle any new project or challenge with enthusiasm; thus, his father was as enthusiastic in supporting Dwan in her Primary calling as she was in fulfilling it.[47] "My dad did not complain about how busy she was and what she was doing," observed Suzanne.[48] While she and Jeff were still at home, Tom and Dwan arranged their travel schedules so that one of them was home with the children. But when Suzanne married and Jeff left to serve his mission in Japan, Tom and Dwan arranged their travel so they would both be gone at the same time and together at home as often as possible. Nevertheless, when Tom had to cook for himself on occasion, he prepared everything in a wok so that he had only one pan to wash.

"I always wished that I could have been in her back pocket," mused her daughter Suzanne, who was twenty years old when her mother became president. "She had so many wonderful experiences. Because she is humble, there were a lot of things we really did not know about, such as the great influence she had on people. When there were conferences or meetings locally, I would try to go hear her speak. I was so proud of her."[49]

A New Mission

In early 1988, Tom received a call to serve as mission president of the Canada Calgary Mission. Dwan was subsequently released at general conference on April 2, 1988, following eight years of service as general Primary president. That July they left for Calgary, where they served for three years. "It was a marvelous experience," Dwan said. "We loved our mission in spite of the hard work. Canada was a special place to serve. We had wonderful missionaries, and there was a strong foundation of the Church there with seventeen stakes, which is unusual for a mission outside of the United States."[50]

Dwan immersed herself in mission life with her characteristic energy and enthusiasm. By choosing to hire cooking help with the allowance provided to operate the mission home, she could be more involved with the missionaries and missionary work. She had a desk in the mission office and went there with Tom every day. At zone conferences, she held a session for the missionaries, instructing them on gospel principles and missionary work. Her gift with music drew missionaries around the piano when they came to the mission home for conferences or in small groups. According to Dwan, "Our missionaries were the best singers in the whole world!"[51]

Dwan's greatest contribution to the mission was her ability to express love to the missionaries. Tom, who claimed he had "the best companion in the world," said, "She has a capacity for love like nobody I have ever met. As she visited with the missionaries, she was an awfully good listener and very empathetic."[52] Brant Taylor, a missionary, stated, "Sister Young has a great spirit and a great knowledge of the gospel and an amazing ability to work and accomplish things. But what I remember most is that whenever she walked in the room, you felt love. It was unlike any other person I have ever been around."[53] Dwan got to know each of the missionaries personally and made thoughtful gestures such as delivering birthday cakes on missionaries' birthdays or dropping off a bag of M&Ms to others to cheer up their day. Of their relationship with the missionaries, Dwan commented, "We've just extended our family."[54]

In May 1990, President Thomas S. Monson called Dwan in Canada with news that the Boy Scouts of America wanted to present her with the Silver Buffalo Award for her many years of service to Scouting. One of her accomplishments while serving as a member of the national Cub Scout Committee was to chair a project to write a booklet to assist families. The Scouting organization was so impressed with this project, in which she suggested that Cub Scout families plan weekly experiences in developing improved caring, sharing, and listening, that they also designated its use by older Scouts and their families. Although it was highly unusual for a mission president and his wife to leave the mission field, President Monson suggested that Dwan and Tom attend the awards ceremonies. They flew to Baltimore, Maryland, and back to Canada in less than twenty-four hours, wanting to be away as short a time as possible.

Dwan missed her family a great deal while they were in the mission field, and they missed her, but the Youngs kept in touch through letters, phone calls, and occasional visits by their children and grandchildren. The ultimate get-together was Tom's surprise party for Dwan's sixtieth birthday. He invited sixty people, including their five children and their spouses, who flew to Calgary, unbeknownst to Dwan. She was overwhelmed and thrilled to see her family, mission staff, and Canadian friends gathered at a restaurant on her birthday.[55]

Challenges and Rewards

While Tom was in the mission field, his sons ran the sign company—the third generation of Youngs to operate it. After his release in July 1991, he returned to the office as a consultant, without the heavy responsibilities of overseeing the day-to-day business. When Michael was asked what his father does at the company, he replied, "Whatever he wants to."[56] Not long after their return from Calgary, Tom and Dwan were in court for a lawsuit brought against them and the company by two disgruntled minority stockholders. Although the case, which had the potential for the dissolution of the sign company, was decided in their favor, nevertheless, the process was both emotionally and financially draining. From this experience Dwan said, "It made us closer as a family and stronger and more reliant on the Lord. We fasted and put our names in the temple and did everything we could do spiritually and put our future in the hands of the Lord. We prayed that we would be able to forgive. I can say that I hold no hard feelings toward them."[57]

With their release and Tom's semi-retirement, the Youngs have been able to spend more time doing what they like best—being with their family. With the number of their grandchildren totalling twenty, Dwan and Tom added on to their home, where they have lived for over thirty years, to accommodate family get-togethers. On Sunday evenings the Young family gathers in the spacious addition for dinner and visiting. The grandchildren look forward to outings at the cabin at Bear Lake just as their parents did. Dwan and Tom cook Thanksgiving dinner at the cabin the day after Thanksgiving so that all the children can come and can also spend the holiday with their in-laws as well. "While we are together as a family, all thirty-two of us," said Michael, "Mom will be off in a corner paying attention one-on-one and really listening to a child. Because she is committed to being a part of her grandchildren's lives, she has a close relationship with each one of them; they are not just part of a crowd of twenty grand-children."[58] Tom noted that their grandchildren, like children he has seen all over the world, are drawn to her. "They can be fussing or crying, and she will pick them up and they will quiet down. She has certain mothering skills that are just marvelous to behold."[59]

"Dwan loves her grandchildren," commented her mother, Vauna. "She spends a lot of time with her grandchildren, especially the younger ones because she was away for three years and she wants them to know her."[60] Christine said, "When we go on trips, she stays at our home and takes care of our children. She says being their mom for a while is the best way to get to know them. Her mother did that often for us, and we are really close to her."[61] Dwan takes each of her grandchildren to lunch and shopping on their birthdays, and, Christine noted, takes their mothers out on their birthdays as well.[62]

Two of the grandchildren have had special needs, as a granddaughter was born without an esophagus and a grandson is developmentally delayed. Dwan, a concerned and caring grandmother, has drawn strength from lessons learned in her own childhood as her family dealt with her brother's limitations. She helps her grandchildren and their parents in handling these challenges by giving extra time to the children and providing a listening ear to their mothers and fathers.

In March 1994, Dwan's ninety-two-year-old mother was in a car accident, which accelerated some problems of aging. For Dwan, who has been very close to her mother all her life, this has been painful to watch. She said, "Although my younger years have been relatively trauma-free, I know this is my test. I struggle as I watch her struggle as she longs to do what she was able to do before. My heart aches for her."[63]

Another facet of Dwan and Tom's post-mission life has been keeping in close touch with their missionaries, who are like family, by hosting reunions at each general conference, attending temple weddings and receptions—sometimes traveling considerable distances to do so—and by visits and phone calls.

Dwan continues to share her energy and leadership in the community and in the Church. For many years Dwan served on the board of Primary Children's Medical Center. She took a leave of absence while she was in Canada, and in January 1993, six months after her return, she became chair of the board of trustees. She also serves on the board of directors of Intermountain Health Care and on the committee for the Church's Pioneer Sesquicentennial Committee, to plan the worldwide celebration for 1997. In her home ward, the Monument Park 15th Ward, she has served as the Primary music leader and, with Tom, as advisers to the young single adults.

A positive, energetic woman with an unusual ability to express love to others, Dwan Jacobsen Young has spent her life in service to others. Whether with her own children or grandchildren, Primary children in the Philippines or Germany, general board members, or the missionaries with whom she labored in Canada, Dwan has felt that "each one is so important," and has endeavored to help many people realize their worth. During her eight-year administration as Primary general president, the Primary underwent dramatic changes in structure and format, and through her able leadership, she helped Church members worldwide catch the vision of the new, international Primary.

8

Michaelene Packer Grassli

1988–1994

I think I was born loving children," said Michaelene Packer Grassli, the eighth Primary general president.[1] A mother of three who wanted a dozen children, Michaelene "was given a whole world full," said Betty Jo N. Jepsen, her counselor and longtime friend.[2] Michaelene's life has been filled with children. As Primary general president, whenever she visited with children, she knelt down, looked into their faces, and talked eye-to-eye, asking them questions about themselves and, particularly, how they would improve Primary, noted her other counselor, Ruth B. Wright.[3] Children who came to her office found a friendly environment and were greeted by a huggable stuffed bear, a whimsical carousel horse, and a smile or hug from Michaelene.

As the eldest child in a family of six and one of the eldest cousins in a large, extended family, as a college coed who majored in home economics, as a young mother whose home was a neighborhood gathering place, and as a Primary leader for most of her adult life, Michaelene Grassli has delighted in children and focused her energy in bettering their lives.

Colonists and Pioneers

On her father's side, Michaelene's roots go back to the early American colonies.[4] Michaelene's ancestor Philip Packer, whose lawyer great-grandfather was believed to have assisted in the King James translation of the Bible, was the first of the Packer family to emigrate from England. He sailed in 1764 and settled in Pennsylvania, where he labored as an indentured servant for four years. Several generations later, Moses Packer and his wife, Eve Williams, both Quakers, moved westward to Ohio.[5] Nathan Williams Packer, one of their twelve children, joined The Church of Jesus Christ of Latter-day Saints, along with his wife, Elizabeth Taylor, in 1833. Nathan and Elizabeth moved westward again, settling in Lehi, Utah, and then Oneida County, Idaho. Their great-grandson Clyde Parkinson Packer, who is Michaelene's grandfather, played basketball for the University of Utah and later coached at Ricks College in Rexburg, Idaho.

Michaelene's Merrill ancestors sailed to America on the *Mayflower*. Her great-great-grandfather moved from New York to Springfield, Illinois, upon joining the Church. The Merrill family watched as the bodies of the Prophet Joseph and Hyrum were brought from Carthage and were part of the exodus from Nauvoo in 1846. The Merrills eventually settled in Cache Valley, Utah, where Michaelene's grandmother, Dora Merrill, was born. She married Clyde Parkinson Packer, and their son, Michaelene's father, Clyde Dean (known as Dean throughout his life), was born March 11, 1916, while Clyde was in Chicago playing in the AAU basketball tournament. When Clyde received news during halftime that his wife had given birth to a baby boy, his teammates chipped in some money and gave the proud new father a ten-dollar gold piece, now a family keepsake.

On her mother's side, Mary Ann Dudley and Edmund Ellsworth, Michaelene's great-great-grandparents, immigrated to Salt Lake City with Brigham Young in 1847. In 1856 President Young appointed Edmund to lead the first handcart company from Iowa City, Iowa, to the Salt Lake Valley. Though the journey was treacherous, Edmund later wrote that he never regretted leaving his "comfortable home, wading streams, crossing high mountains, and pulling through heavy sand," so his family could "hear a prophet's voice and live with the Saints of God."[6]

In 1847, the same year that the pioneers arrived in the Salt Lake Valley, another set of Michaelene's maternal great-great-grandparents, George and Mary Hamilton McKinlay, and several of their children joined the Church in their native Scotland. Inasmuch as George was a miner with a large family and little money, he sent one of his sons to America to earn passage for the rest of the family.

George and Mary's son Robert McKinlay, who is Michaelene's great-grandfather, married Isabella Wausen, a nonmember, in 1854. She was baptized later that same year. "When the missionaries first came to her house," related Michaelene's mother, Dottie McKinlay Packer, "she offered them tea and when they didn't drink tea, she said, 'Out you go. If you can't drink my tea, you can't stay in my house.' But they finally convinced her it was not anything personal; it was a gospel principle."[7]

Archibald, the eleventh of Robert and Isabella McKinlay's thirteen children and Michaelene's grandfather, was born in Lindsay Place, Fifeshire, Scotland, and immigrated with his family to Utah in 1875. He married Susannah Louiette Stephens from Menan, Idaho, in 1916. Their daughter Dottie Marguerite McKinlay married Clyde Dean Packer in the Salt Lake Temple in 1937.

Childhood Memories

Susan Michaelene Packer, Dottie and Dean's first child, was born in Salt Lake City, Utah, on June 19, 1940. At the time of Michaelene's birth, her father was a medical student at the University of Utah. While Dean completed his medical degree, surgical internship, and residency, the Packers moved several times—to Colorado, North Carolina, and Washington. Moving frequently didn't bother Michaelene, for she later said, "I didn't know any differently. It wasn't traumatic. Maybe that's one of the reasons that I'm adaptable and open-minded. But perhaps as a result of our family's moving, I didn't form close childhood relationships outside my home. My family was the center of my life."[8] Dottie made moving an adventure for the family. She would say, "Oh, you'll have new friends, and we'll have a new house, and it will be interesting. We'll find the Church, and everything's going to be wonderful."[9] This trait of looking at the bright side of things was passed from mother to daughter, for Michaelene, throughout her life, has been known for her optimistic, positive attitude.

Because organized branches of the Church were not always available in the areas where they lived, the Packers often had to hunt up Church members during those transitional years. In Greensboro, North Carolina, they didn't find any Church members until they wrote to Church headquarters in Salt Lake City. They were informed that one other Latter-day Saint family, the John Stevenses, lived in the area and had been holding a home Sunday School. The two families rented a hall, posted signs at the Air Force base about Church meetings, and held Sunday School. From that small beginning, the Church has since grown to several stakes within the same area.

When Michaelene was in the fifth grade, the family settled in Blackfoot, Idaho, where Dean established a surgical practice. Later, as an adult reflecting on her life in Blackfoot, Michaelene felt that the Church members she knew there lived close to the Lord and "were not fettered by a lot of the things of the world."[10]

Michaelene and her younger sister, Deanne, enjoyed helping their mother take care of younger brothers Allan, Richard, and Kelly. Brent, a fourth brother, died at birth in 1956. Four years later, when Michaelene was twenty and attending Brigham Young University, her youngest brother, Norris, was born. Michaelene didn't just baby-sit her brothers. She involved them in creative and often productive activities and once even convinced Richard, who was five at the time, to become "a clean-up fairy" by dressing him in a tutu.[11]

Deanne and Michaelene shared a room and occasionally disagreed about who was occupying too much space. Once, to their mother's dismay, they drew a line with a crayon down the middle of the bed to designate their respective sides. When they were a little older, their parents built a new home, with a separate bedroom for each girl, but that lasted for only one night—they missed each other too much.[12]

In the Packer family, Michaelene and Deanne, who were twenty-one months apart, were known as "the girls," and the four brothers were known as "the boys." "The girls" often swam together in the canal or climbed an apple tree in the orchard, eating green apples. Deanne said, "Part of what enriched our childhood was our cousins"[13]—Lyn and Josie, who were near their age and who lived nearby. The four girls often visited Grandma Packer together, playing princess or dress-up in her two-story house, which was, in their eyes, an enchanting place.

Michaelene and Deanne were best friends growing up, never having more than "an occasional tiff," recalled Deanne. "I grew up feeling good about myself because my adored older sister treated me like I was an important person. She included me when I wanted to go with her and her friends and was considerate of my feelings in those circumstances. She didn't make disparaging remarks to me, such as, 'you're dumb' or 'you're ugly,' or make me feel inadequate. Rather, she encouraged me and told me that 'I could do it.'"[14]

"Michaelene has been a pleasant, happy person all her life," said her mother, Dottie. "Teachers liked Michaelene, who was a good student, and recognized leadership qualities in her. (She was a class officer three years in high school.) As a young child, she developed an ability to express herself and to get her point across—sometimes refusing to let up even when I no longer wanted to discuss an issue."[15]

Dean Packer served as a bishop, a high councilor, and as a member of a stake presidency while maintaining a demanding medical practice. Dottie served in Primary, YMMIA, and Relief Society and later served as a Church curriculum writer. Even though her parents, especially her father, were busy, Michaelene felt she had a loving, warm relationship with them and that they generously gave her their time.[16] Her favorite memory of her father is of sitting on his lap and having his arms around her. That image and feeling of fatherly love would have significance in Michaelene's adult life. Another happy memory is of him singing "double forte"—very loud in musical terms—whenever he returned home from his office or church meetings.[17] Michaelene remembered discussions around the dinner table, at family nights, and at her bedside about Heavenly Father and Jesus Christ.[18]

"My mother can do anything she decides to do—whether it is teaching Gospel Doctrine or learning Spanish and computers in her seventies—because she is capable, positive, and energetic," stated Michaelene, "and she does it all with a passion for excellence. As a child, I didn't hear complaints from Mother about my father's obligations away from the family. It was a matter of course. When we were together it was wonderful, but when he wasn't home, we went ahead and had dinner. I didn't hear her say, 'He's never home.' She just did what needed to be done. She's also very witty, and often defused a potentially difficult situation with humor. Some of my pleasant memories of her are of canning fruit together on summer days and talking about some of the important aspects of life. From my mother, I learned there is usually a better way to do things."[19]

As the eldest grandchild on both sides of her family, Michaelene enjoyed close relationships with her grandparents and extended family. Her Packer grandparents lived nearby in Rexburg, while her McKinlay grandparents lived in Richfield, Utah. Trips to Richfield were some of Michaelene's favorite vacations, although she recalled that "with four children in the car before the days of air conditioning, driving long distances in the summer was not a lot of fun."[20] Her Grandfather McKinlay often used to quote James Russell Lowell, who said, "Be noble, and the nobleness in others, sleeping, but never dead, will rise in majesty to meet thine own."[21] It is a memory of her grandfather that her mother has kept alive, and Michaelene quotes it often.

An avid reader, Michaelene said, "I loved to read in my bed at night or in the backyard on a blanket. I'd get some raisins or I'd make cookies of graham crackers and frosting to eat while I was reading, and I would read for as long as I could keep my eyes open."[22] One of her favorite books was Louisa May Alcott's *Little Women.*

Drawing and painting fascinated Michaelene. In grade school her friends often asked her to draw paper dolls and clothes for them. Her grandmother, Louiette McKinlay, was a watercolor artist and introduced Michaelene to watercolors. In her first lesson, she helped her granddaughter paint a wild rose. But more lasting was her teaching Michaelene to observe nature closely. Michaelene remembered, "She got me to kneel right down and look at things. She pointed out the face on a pansy. Her observations of nature became part of me because my mother, her daughter, did the same thing. She would say to us children, 'Run quick. Look at this beautiful thing. Look at that blue jay, see how the coloring is. Look at the beauty of the bare winter trees silhouetted against the sunset. They are lacy black lines against gorgeous color.'"[23]

Michaelene also excelled in music. She said, "I didn't know I was going to like singing, but when I was in the ninth grade, our school put on an operetta. I tried out and got the lead. Mother was surprised because as she had heard me singing around the house when I was a little girl, she thought I didn't carry a tune very well." After the operetta was over, Michaelene continued to sing in groups and performed solos. "I always envisioned myself as a musical comedy star," she noted.[24] Her sister, Deanne, often accompanied her on the piano when she sang soprano solos or performed in ensembles at Church meetings or school programs. Deanne and Michaelene were comfortable telling each other what they thought would improve the performance. Deanne said, "I learned to sense her breathing and her expression. We would go over and over music. We were really trying to perfect pieces as a team; it wasn't just 'hurry up and do this.' Michaelene had a beautiful, clear voice."[25]

But more than literature, art, and music, Michaelene loved children. She said, "One of my earliest recollections is of loving babies and wanting to be with them. As the oldest cousin in both my mother's and father's families, and the oldest of six siblings, I had plenty of experience with children of all ages as I was growing up."[26]

Even though Michaelene had an idyllic childhood, as she entered her teen years, she experienced the struggles of most adolescents—a search for identity and acceptance. Michaelene recalled, "I remember always feeling that I was different, but I think nearly every child feels that. I envied the cheerleaders, but I didn't try out because I didn't think it was in the realm of possibility for me.

"It doesn't matter that I wasn't a cheerleader. I can see now that what I didn't get from my school experiences I did get in the Church. I had leads in two stake plays and participated in a speech contest, road shows, dance festivals, and an all-Church choir. Those great opportunities helped build my self-esteem and feelings of competence and feelings of belonging in the Church. Activities conducted by caring leaders gave me much of what I needed.

"I remember how I thought that anything bad that happened in high school was the end of the world. I had fun doing some dating, but I didn't have a date to my own junior prom, and I was one who had spent all the time decorating for the dance. My very best friend was the queen of the prom."[27] Deanne remembered her sister's experience in another way. "Michaelene was cheerful and loving and very well liked," she said, "and she did have her fair share of dates."[28]

Family Life

Following her graduation from Blackfoot High School, Michaelene enrolled at Brigham Young University, where she majored in home economics education with an emphasis on child development. When she was a junior, Michaelene met and began dating a Swiss convert to the Church, Leonard Grassli. During that school year, their relationship deepened, and they became engaged. Michaelene and Leonard M Grassli were married in the Idaho Falls Temple on July 28, 1961. After living a few months in Provo, they moved to Ogden, where Leonard and a partner established a landscape architecture business. (Later, he transferred his company to Salt Lake City.) Michaelene did not continue with college as she wanted to have a family right away; in fact, she even "ordered a dozen" children.

The first Christmas after their marriage, Michaelene and Leonard spent Christmas Eve with her family. They combined their creative efforts and made her two-year-old brother, Norris, a playhouse out of a large washing machine box, fashioning it into a Swiss chalet. That play box became Norris's favorite toy, and he gave it up only when he outgrew the box. Subsequently, when the Grasslis had their own children, they made another play box that the girls enjoyed for years.[29]

Michaelene and Leonard's first child, Jane Anne, was born in 1963, and their second child, Susan, the following year. Over the next five years, Michaelene worried that they would not have another child but rejoiced when Sara was born in 1970. Her mother remembers visiting Michaelene and Sara in the hospital and seeing Michaelene crying with joy over her new daughter and saying, "I didn't think I would ever have any more children."[30] One of Michaelene's disappointments in life has been that her dream of having a large family was not fulfilled. Although she would have liked more children, she said, "The three who were sent to us on this earth have been a source of wonder and joy and learning."[31] Perhaps this longing further turned her heart to children.

For many years, the Grassli family lived in North Ogden and then in Pleasant View, a small community a few miles north of Ogden. Michaelene, Leonard, and the girls enjoyed swimming, skiing, and camping together. Art also played a big part in their lives. With art supplies on hand and two artistic parents, the girls had ample opportunity to draw and paint. Susan remembered her mother giving impromptu art lessons in the backyard to her and several of her friends. She encouraged them to work with different media, such as watercolor, charcoal, and crayon, and helped them make sand candles and experiment with batik. In the backyard she also wrote stories with her children.[32] Michaelene and her daughters did lots of "crafty things" and sewed and cooked together. She often designed and sewed the girls' prom dresses as well as many other professional-looking items of clothing. "The fact that I majored in home economics shows where my interests are," stated Michaelene. "Women have so many contributions to make. I've felt a great personal reward and joy in the kinds of things I've chosen to do."[33]

The Grasslis' backyard was a neighborhood gathering place. With Leonard's expertise as a landscape architect, their yard was "beautiful but playable," commented Betty Jo N. Jepsen, a backyard neighbor who later served as Michaelene's counselor. "The children could just enjoy it with swings, a playhouse, sandbox, trails through the flower gardens for them to ride their trikes, a big inner tube to jump on, and a picnic table available for picnics or performances. The neighborhood children congregated at the Grasslis' home, and they were always welcome. Michaelene was a generous mother in allowing them to get into the dress-up box, the makeup box, the cookie makings, the paint makings, and the bubble blowing."[34] Susan's friends told her "she was lucky to have such a nice mom." She said, "We had the house where everybody wanted to come play. I would have creative and fun birthday parties. One year we wore aprons my mom had made and created something with play dough. Another year we made our own pizzas."[35] Sara loved the celebrations her mother planned. "On the morning of your birthday, you'd walk down to the kitchen, which was completely decorated with crepe paper and balloons. On Valentine's Day, the table was decorated all in red, and she would make pink, heart-shaped pancakes. She would have a little gift in a box on our plates."[36]

"I have all wonderful memories of her," said Jane Anne, her oldest daughter. "One of my very favorite things about growing up was that she read to us in bed—stories like *The Secret Garden.*" Other favorite memories were their Swiss Christmas traditions, which included playing Swiss music throughout the season and having real candles on the tree.[37]

Morning scripture study was a frequent event at the Grassli home. "I appreciate the climate in our home, and I have to give my husband credit for making such a loving atmosphere possible," said Michaelene.[38] Susan recalled that family home evening was "a big deal." Whether it was preparing the lesson or fixing the dessert, "Mom said to us, 'This is your assignment. What kind of help do you need to do it?'"[39] Part of the evening included a discussion of the coming week's events and particularly, according to Susan, "What can we do to help Mom do her Primary work and still keep the house running?"[40] As the girls grew up and left home, the Grassli family has continued holding family home evenings together. On the first Monday of the month, the extended family meets for dinner and a short lesson.

Michaelene and Leonard have had a very happy marriage, which has developed over the years as they have both worked to make their relationship successful. Michaelene said that they have had to learn to communicate effectively and that "sometimes we have to agree that we will disagree."[41] Their daughter Susan said, "To anyone who comes across the two of them, it's obvious the kind of relationship they have. Mom absolutely adores my father, and he adores her. They have a very deep and substantive love, respect, and admiration for each other. They're each other's friend. Every relationship has its obstacles, and theirs does, too. I don't think they would have the relationship they do without some struggles."[42]

Dwan J. Young, who served with Michaelene in the Primary for many years, noted, "Michaelene has a husband who absolutely idolizes her. When she is hesitant about doing something, he says, 'Come on, Michaelene, you can do it.' He is her cheerleader and best supporter. I think a lot of her being able to do what she does is his support."[43]

"I have been very blessed to have love in my life," said Michaelene. "I realize that doesn't come to everybody. My marriage has been what could be called a crowning point in my life. Leonard's love and encouragement, his pride in my work, and his unselfish support of my responsibilities—even through his years as a bishop—have allowed me to increase my abilities and expand my capacity. I am able to do as I have because of him."[44]

Building on a Firm Foundation

Though she grew up in a home where her parents were always active in the Church, held responsible callings, and later served four missions, and though her own home with Leonard as a partner has had the Church as one of its chief cornerstones, Michaelene has had to develop and nourish her own testimony. This has come as she has studied the gospel and applied its principles in her life and as she has participated and served in Church activities and programs.

"I always knew Mother would tell me the truth," Michaelene said. "She taught Book of Mormon to twelve- and thirteen-year-olds in Sunday School when she was only fourteen and throughout her life has had a firm testimony of our Heavenly Father and the Savior. That legacy of faith from both my parents is the foundation upon which my own testimony grew."[45]

One of her earliest experiences in studying a principle and learning how it related to her own life came when she was eight years old and gave a talk in Sunday School about the pre-earth life. "My mother helped me prepare for it," she recalled. "We talked about the war in heaven and the choices we made. I was really impressed with the fact that we chose to follow the plan our Savior stood for—our Heavenly Father's plan—and that Satan would be happy and would rejoice if we made choices that took us away from our Heavenly Father.

"I remember thinking, 'Satan is not going to rejoice over me! If I climbed into bed without saying my prayers, I would think, 'If I don't pray, Satan will rejoice—and I'm not going to let him.' Although I've made plenty of mistakes, that feeling has stayed with me through the years and has colored how I've reacted to many situations."[46]

One day Michaelene's Primary teacher invited the class to her house, where they learned to make hot chocolate and cinnamon toast. Michaelene especially remembered walking on top of the crusty snow and how bright and sunny the winter day was. Thinking of how delicious the snack tasted, she said, "I thought of learning something that common in the context of Primary and thought my Heavenly Father cares about more than religious matters. He cares about all parts of us, the everyday things, too. He wants us to learn how to do many things that are interesting and useful—like how to be nourished."[47]

"I was blessed with a believing heart," said Michaelene. "From my earliest years I have believed in and loved my Heavenly Father and his son, Jesus Christ. As my testimony matured, I have had questions arise in my mind. Then a hymn, a scripture, a lesson, or words of a family member or friend would trigger thoughts and impressions that either resolved my questions or resulted in a peaceful feeling of comfort through the Spirit. My faith is reaffirmed repeatedly through these experiences."[48]

She received her first Church calling—as the Junior Sunday School secretary—when she was fourteen. As an adult, she held many positions in the Church on both ward and stake levels, including drama director and counselor in YWMIA and teacher and stake president in Primary. Her artistic and musical talents served her well as a director of road shows, where she created imaginative and captivating scenery and costumes, wrote clever scripts, and made the experience enthralling for her children to watch. Whatever Michaelene's calling or responsibilities, her daughter Susan observed, "She always gave one hundred percent."[49] "If we only dip a toe in the Church," Michaelene explained, "we can't even begin to know what opportunities there are for our personal and temporal growth as well as our spiritual growth. We need to jump in full force with both feet."[50]

When Michaelene was called at age thirty-one as president of the Pleasant View Stake Primary, she said she cried for two days because she felt she couldn't do it. But while attending a Primary conference in Salt Lake City in 1971, she was thrilled by the power with which general president LaVern W. Parmley spoke. When LaVern challenged the Primary leaders with the words, "Increase your capacity," Michaelene thought to herself, "Yes, I can do that."[51] As a result, she gained an ability to cope with her responsibility and more confidence that she could receive inspiration and plan a stake leadership meeting every month, although she said, "It scared me to death to stand up in front of a group and conduct a meeting." Motivated by Sister Parmley's words to expand her abilities, she tried out new ideas, such as a two-screen slide presentation.[52]

After a three-year period of service in the stake Primary, Michaelene had an experience that she later realized helped prepare her for general Church callings. "One night I was reading an *Ensign* article about Church leaders in Europe," she wrote in her journal. "While I was reading, a wave of love washed over me for Saints around the world. It was a new feeling—an expanding of my vision of the Church and an increase of my capacity to love. I started to cry. I sense now that the Spirit was blessing me in preparation for future service."[53] Michaelene's life took a surprising new turn when Naomi M. Shumway, who succeeded LaVern Parmley as general president of the Primary, chose Michaelene to serve on the Primary general board and assigned her to the Scout committee.

Finding Joy in Serving the Lord

Dwan J. Young was called in 1980 as the general Primary president and asked that Michaelene serve as her second counselor. When President Spencer W. Kimball extended this call to Michaelene, she asked him if he had any counsel for her. She recalled, "He looked at me seriously and said, 'Yes, I would counsel you to find joy in serving the Lord.' Those are words I frequently recall and repeat in many settings. I know our service can bring us joy as our faith in the Lord Jesus Christ increases."[54]

Michaelene's daughters were still quite young when she was called to the Primary general presidency. "I was delighted with the response of our children when Leonard read them the letter from the First Presidency that confirmed my call," said Michaelene. "The girls began squealing and asking all kinds of questions, before he could even finish. They were very pleased and anxious to help."[55] Nevertheless, balancing her family, home, and Church work presented challenges, but

Michaelene, in her typical fashion, minimized the difficulties and instead chose to focus on the way Primary enriched their lives. She just knew it would all work out and had faith that the Lord would "make her equal" to all her tasks. Jane Anne felt her mother's calling was a great blessing to all of them, particularly for her when President Marion G. Romney, a counselor in the First Presidency, set Michaelene apart. "I had an overwhelming feeling that our Heavenly Father knew me personally," Jane Anne recalled. "That was something I'll never forget, a wonderful experience."[56] Sara, the youngest daughter, who was five when her mother was called to the general board, said, "I've never seen her hold a regular ward calling. Mom is Primary to me. My fondest memory is Primary."[57]

The new presidency, which also included Virginia Beesley Cannon as first counselor, was sustained on April 5, 1980, at general conference. Michaelene's assignment was to oversee CTR and Valiant classes, Cub Scouting, in-service training, and audiovisual materials. During her service on the National Cub Scout Committee, she received the Silver Beaver and Silver Antelope Awards.

Dwan Young commented about working with Michaelene: "I had an opportunity to work with her on the Blazer Committee, so we had experience in the early days together. She is a very capable, creative woman. We used to laugh in our presidency because we had two left-brained people and one right-brained person. Virginia Cannon and I are very focused and, I would say for me, too restrictive in my vision. Michaelene is not restricted at all. She sees the whole picture. Nothing that has been done before encumbers her at all. She is able to put everything out and start afresh and try different approaches. I just admire that so much in her. I kept telling her we needed her because she gave a totally different perspective to everything."[58]

The Eighth General President

In late 1987, Leonard told Michaelene he felt impressed that she would be called as the next Primary general president.

She replied, "Oh, don't talk about that." A person focused on what the Lord directs and not one to worry about what's going to happen, she said, "I did not really allow myself to think about it."[59]

On March 8, 1988, Michaelene and Leonard met with President Thomas S. Monson, Second Counselor in the First Presidency. He extended a call to Michaelene to serve as the general president of the Primary. She said her first inclination was to "shrink because each of us knows our own inabilities more than anybody else does. But by that time, I was more mature in Church service and, unlike when I was called as stake Primary president, it didn't throw me emotionally. I had confidence that the Lord would sustain me as he does those whom he calls. My own personal inadequacies would be compensated for."[60]

"President Monson was very, very considerate in every aspect of the call," Michaelene said. "Because of his caring and thorough manner, I had a sense of the trust the Lord had in me and also that of the First Presidency. I could not have underestimated the significance of this call because of the way I was nurtured and guided and counseled by President Monson and members of the Twelve through that time."[61]

Michaelene's sister, Deanne, knew that Michaelene was humbled and feeling inadequate about her new responsibility. But Michaelene told her, "I know if our Father in Heaven has enough confidence in me to call me to this, then he will make me equal to the task."[62]

When Dwan Young was released to serve a mission with her husband, Michaelene was sustained as the eighth general Primary president at general conference on April 2, 1988. Betty Jo Nelson Jepsen and Ruth Broadbent Wright were sustained as her counselors. At the time of their calling, 1.3 million children were enrolled in Primary. The general board consisted of fifteen members.

Michaelene and her counselors retained the Primary curriculum based on the scriptures, including the Articles of Faith, which they regarded as "strong" and which helped "children learn more and understand more about the gospel of Jesus

Christ at an earlier age than ever before."[63] Because of rapidly declining moral standards in the world and the wide exposure to them that children receive just by living in the world, especially by viewing television and movies, Michaelene felt that children must confront moral issues at a younger age and suggested they be taught the principles in the pamphlet *For the Strength of Youth.*

In 1988, the Primary reduced the children's sacrament meeting presentation from a sixteen-page booklet to a nine-page guideline. It was further simplified in 1991 to a two-page outline rather than a detailed script, allowing local Primaries to develop programs to meet their own needs. Michaelene said, "Although it appeared we were adding further responsibilities to already busy Primary presidencies and some leaders felt they needed a script from us, having them develop the program made it more meaningful for the children because the experiences and testimonies were their own. For the 1991 program, 'I Can Develop a Testimony of Jesus Christ,' what was presented in each ward or branch were the feelings and testimonies of their children! The sacrament meeting program was also thus applicable on any unit level worldwide."[64]

In 1989, after ten years of development, the Church published the *Children's Songbook,* a new illustrated songbook to delight children visually as well as musically. It included favorite songs and new songs written for the book, all focusing on gospel principles. "I don't think the Church has published anything more lovely than this songbook," Michaelene said. "It was intended for families to use in their homes as well as for use in Primary. It does what the rest of the world can't do for children, but what we do best—teach the gospel."[65]

As the Primary presidency and general board members conducted leadership training both at Church headquarters and at regional meetings, they taught principles, strengthened local leaders, and helped them become more spiritually self-reliant. Michaelene's exceptional ability to communicate touched many Primary leaders' lives as she presented messages to them. One stake leader wrote, "While we have considered the handbook to be the vital backbone of Primary leadership, your talks have

been to us the heart. Your talk 'What Is Best for the Children?'
is a classic. I regularly reread it to recommit myself to children
(including my own) and to doing for them what the Savior
would do for them if He were here. Thank you for helping us
feel of the Savior's love through your testimony and teaching
these many years."[66] Other leaders appreciated her enthusiasm,
charm, and wisdom.[67]

As the Primary presidency discussed needs and made
decisions, they did so with the worldwide church in mind. "We
concentrated on the whole world," Ruth Wright said. "When we
considered anything, we asked, How is this going to work in
Guatemala, in China, in India, or Pleasant View, Utah? We tried
to teach principles that are true for all God's children."[68] Primary
lesson manuals were subsequently revised, with more emphasis on principles and more alternatives in implementation.

Focus on Children

When the new Primary presidency met for the first time,
they discussed focusing on children rather than on programs.
Ruth Wright, second counselor, recalled, "We thought the program should support the children, and we really wanted to
look at children in a different way. We wanted people to look
at children, love them, and plan what is really best for the
child. It was a great process for us to go through, and it took
us a while to identify our philosophy in words, to define and
create solid statements. Our training in regions and presentations to the Brethren was based on these goals: regard children, teach children, activate children, and help children
prepare for baptism, the priesthood, and temple blessings."[69]

The Primary presidency's efforts culminated in August
1993, when the First Presidency launched Focus on Children.
In a letter sent to general and local authorities, they stated, "We
reemphasize the need for all adult members of the Church to
focus on our children in an ongoing effort to help them learn
to follow the teachings of the Savior. . . . Because this responsibility for our children is so important, we must rededicate ourselves to nourish and bless them temporally and spiritually."[70]

The First Presidency outlined four goals to help members focus on children: (1) Teach members to recognize the worth of children; (2) Identify and invite each child; (3) Give children high-quality gospel teaching; (4) Ensure that children receive gospel ordinances. "The mission of the Church includes the children," Michaelene stated. "We are to invite all to come unto Christ—including children."[71]

"Behold Your Little Ones," a First Presidency satellite broadcast, was presented throughout the Church on January 23, 1994. President Gordon B. Hinckley, President Thomas S. Monson, Elder M. Russell Ballard of the Quorum of the Twelve, and Michaelene each spoke about focusing on and valuing children. Michaelene asked that Church members understand, listen and be kind to, and teach the gospel to children.[72] Segments of a new video, *Teach the Child*, were shown as part of the broadcast. The video, for use by all who have an influence on children—parents, grandparents, Primary teachers and leaders, and other adults—was released in February. Michaelene stated of the general presidency's efforts in behalf of children, "If even just a fraction of our dream for what can happen comes to be, I will feel satisfied."[73]

"As I watched the satellite broadcast, I thought about Michaelene's marvelous ability to speak and communicate her ideas," said her brother Kelly Packer. "She is very energetic and lively when she talks. She communicates her ideas in a way that is not boring, yet not overly pretentious, in more of a suggesting, loving way. But it is effective in making a point."[74]

Following the introduction of Focus on Children, Michaelene felt that she witnessed throughout the Church a "turning of the hearts of the fathers to the children" as she saw examples of stake and ward conferences focusing on children, bishoprics and ward councils evaluating what children need and how Primary can be strengthened, family home evening fairs, and an emphasis on better gospel instruction in homes. "The concept of turning the hearts of the children to the fathers has been around a long time," Michaelene said, "but Focus on Children is bringing to bear the other half of Malachi 4:6, that the hearts of the fathers be turned to the children."[75]

A Creative Leadership Style

Because Leonard's landscape business is located in Salt Lake City, the Grasslis often made the hour-long commute together from their home in Pleasant View while Michaelene was president. Leonard said, "I heard her talks over and over as we drove. She worked hard at that; she didn't just throw them together. One of her leadership skills is that she never worries about who gets the credit. She also listens to people. I attended the Philmont Scout training camp in New Mexico fourteen years with her, and people just swarmed around her because she listened to them. She listened to her board members, and they felt free to express their opinions."[76]

"My philosophy of leadership," said Michaelene, "was to surround myself with a rich mix of women with diverse experience, talents, and personalities, to listen carefully to them, help them see the big picture, establish a direction, give them some guidelines, and turn them loose! This process proved to be very productive in our cause for children."[77]

"She was open to all new ideas," stated Betty Jo Jepsen. "She was never threatened by a better or a new idea. Whenever she prepared a message, she asked our advice in how she could strengthen it. She didn't care who got credit— she just wanted whatever was in process to be a wonderful product."[78]

Ruth Wright said, "We worked really hard, but we had a wonderful time working together. We laughed; we cried. She seldom gave her opinion first; often we had to say, 'Now, how do you feel?' She listened to what others said. She didn't move ahead until we were all in agreement. And sometimes we were not all in agreement."[79]

Michaelene trained board members through weekly meetings, travel assignments, and through "an ongoing dialogue," according to former board member Virginia Pearce. "We would receive a whole assignment rather than a piece of it so we could understand as much as we could about what we were doing."[80] In between intense two-hour workshops at leadership retreats, the Primary board often played children's games such as hopscotch and jump rope, and they delighted in each other's company. Their final meeting together as a board ended with their blowing bubbles in a meadow.

Michaelene's zest for life was evident in her leadership and contagious to those who served with her. "She is an alive person," said Virginia Pearce. "If I had to choose one adjective to describe Michaelene, it would be her sense of aliveness—a delight in life and adventure and people and new things. She really has an artist's soul and a keen sense of appreciation for beauty. It's fun to be around someone like that."[81] Ruth Wright observed, "Michaelene took very seriously the responsibility of being the general Primary president, but she didn't take herself seriously."[82] One board member noted, "She can make weird faces. Every now and then we got a look at her weird faces during board meetings. She is energetic, charming, and fun."[83]

Michaelene experienced challenges as she served. She found driving to Salt Lake City every day to be exhausting, particularly during the winter of 1983–84 when the Wasatch Front was inundated with record snowfalls. One evening as she arrived home after driving for months on roads that were almost impassable with snow, she drove into her garage and started to cry, saying to herself, "I don't want to do this."[84] But characteristically, Michaelene generally looked at the positive side of driving as thinking and planning time.

Michaelene's nearly twenty years of experience in giving worldwide Primary service profoundly affected her. "I am a different person," she said in an interview while she was president. "I think I would always have been faithful, but these experiences have given me a sense of the scope of the mission of the Church and a deep and abiding commitment to that mission. I will always remember seeing children in one meeting after another in South America and the Philippines all dressed in white and hearing them sing the Primary songs for leaders who had come for training. In any country, I cannot hear the familiar songs in unfamiliar words without a deepened sense of what the gospel of Jesus Christ means to the world.

"We need to get beyond the cultural aspects of the Church and not expect all Primaries to be like those in the western United States. The Church is worldwide; what is important is teaching children how to return to their Heavenly Father."[85]

Her association with the General Authorities for twenty years strengthened her testimony of the gospel and the mission of the Church. "I have great trust in the prophets, seers, and revelators and other General Authorities who lead our church," she said. "Each brings his unique perspective into a rich mix of talents and experience. In my observation, they may have many different viewpoints and management styles, but they are united on doctrine and direction. I do admire and respect these brilliant and spiritually gifted men, and I am honored to associate with them. We have tried scrupulously as a presidency to follow their counsel and direction.

"I know God lives, that Jesus Christ is our Savior, and the fulness of the gospel is on the earth today. The Church of Jesus Christ of Latter-day Saints is the kingdom of God on earth and is led by latter-day prophets."[86]

Focus on Family

Although Michaelene was involved in Primary service on the general level from 1975 to 1994, her family life was what she hoped and planned it to be—joyous and closely knit. While she served on the general board and her young daughters were in school, she made certain that she was home when they arrived home from school. She didn't want them coming home to an empty house.[87]

Her five grandchildren call her "Grandma G," and she says, "These little grandchildren are like dessert to me—they can be enjoyed openly and enthusiastically in all their sweetness. . . . They lift my spirits, spice my life with joy, and generate in me great hope for the future."[88] She spends a lot of time with her grandchildren, but since they live in Salt Lake City, sixty miles away from her home in Pleasant View, she hungers to be with children and says she often needs to have "a kid fix." One Christmas she and Leonard held a neighborhood Christmas party at their home and included all the children in the neighborhood. Another time the doorbell rang and an eight-year-old neighbor girl said, "I came to visit. I thought maybe you were missing children and would like to have a child come and visit you."[89]

Michaelene also has experienced a joyful association with her extended family. The Packers hold a two-day family reunion every other summer. For one of these get-togethers Michaelene brought fabric, batting, and quilt frames. All those who helped tie the quilt—including men, boys, and children— participated in a drawing to win the quilt. Her parents' home in Provo often has been the gathering place for Sunday night visits. Michaelene, according to her mother, "made a great effort, as busy as she was as Primary president, to attend family functions, whether it was a shower or wedding reception or funeral."[90]

New Adventures

Following six and one-half years of service as Primary general president, Michaelene was released October 1, 1994, at general conference, with "no regrets" and with the feeling that her presidency "accomplished what we set out to do in heightening awareness of the needs of children in the Church."[91] She then wrote a history of her years in Primary, served as a visiting teacher, volunteered as a reading aide in an inner-city Ogden school, and anticipated continued Church service. Refocusing on her love of singing, she successfully auditioned for the Mormon Tabernacle Choir in the spring of 1995.

Although Michaelene continued with her art experiences and managed to fit in a watercolor class on occasion while she was president, she enjoyed having more time following her release to pursue these interests as well as to take vocal lessons. "I love contemplating doing some things in art and music as well learning to use a computer," Michaelene said shortly after she became a "civilian" again. "I am energized by change, and since I have had several lives on 'hold' for twenty years, I can hardly decide what to do first. I will always be busy doing something. But it is very easy to get caught up in doing fun things. There is much good work to be done in the kingdom, and that is always most important. It is delightful to have more time to spend with the children and to read. I have more relaxed time and can go to bed being comfortably tired instead of totally exhausted."[92]

"People may think of my life as idyllic," said Michaelene. "That I have not had a hard life has been a disappointment to some. Nevertheless, I have had my challenges—and I am not dead yet! I know that we all will have our refining fire. Sometimes when I have been discouraged, I think of going back and sitting on my daddy's lap and having his arms around me. That's one of the reasons why it is so easy for me to envision our Heavenly Father. But I have been blessed with a happy heart and I tend to minimize the tragedy or trials in my life. I believe what Abraham Lincoln said, 'A man is about as happy as he makes up his mind to be.' And one of the blessings of agency is we can choose to be happy. I do choose to be happy."[93]

Michaelene Packer Grassli has spent her life loving children young and old, has focused her energy on teaching them the gospel of Jesus Christ, and, as an extraordinary Primary leader for twenty years, has fervently shared her vision of heavenly love with those who influence children.

9

Patricia Peterson Pinegar
1994–

*P*at Pinegar gathered her grandchildren around her in a special family meeting. Each grandchild wore a hat decorated with a sunflower. Pat began the lesson by helping each child say the word *tenacious*. Then she said, "Sunflowers are tenacious. Last summer I noticed a sunflower growing out of a crack in a sidewalk. Can you imagine how hard it was for that sunflower to grow in a tiny crack in cement? Not only was this sunflower growing, it was blooming. That sunflower was tenacious. Tenacious means you never give up; you never stop trying to do your best. In the morning, the flower turned to face the rising sun. It followed the sunlight all day long and by evening it had turned clear around to face the setting sun. Sunlight helped it survive. With your sunflower hat, you are like that sunflower. Who is the light we must follow?"

The answer came: "Jesus."

"That's right," said Pat. "Jesus is the source of light we must follow. By obeying his commandments, we are following his light and he will lead us safely home."

Now when the Pinegar grandchildren wear their sunflower hats or see them in their bedrooms, they remember the story of the tenacious sunflower growing out of a crack in the cement. They remember that it turned its face to follow the light, and they remember that they must turn and follow Jesus and never give up even when things are hard.

Patricia P. Pinegar's life has been filled with moments like this. As mother of eight, she has often been surrounded by children teaching them. "I love children," says Pat. "I love holding tiny babies and feeling that I have the ability as a mother to comfort and take care of them and love them and nurture them. I delight in every little thing children do, every step they take, and every word they say."[1]

A Pioneer Heritage

Pat was the second child of four children born to Laurence and Wavie Williams Peterson: Larry, Pat, David, and Laurelee. Wavie met Laurence, or "Pete" as she called him, in Cedar City, Utah, in November 1932. They quickly fell in love and eloped two months later to Las Vegas, Nevada. At the time, Wavie was teaching school, and since married women were not allowed to teach, the Petersons decided to keep their marriage a secret. But someone found out about the wedding and five days later, the headlines in the Cedar City newspaper said "Local Couple Weds in Nevada." Depression poverty didn't stop everyone from celebrating the marriage. Wavie's fellow teachers draped her in a lace curtain veil and paraded the newlyweds all over Cedar City in a one-horse shay. The sympathetic school superintendent allowed Wavie to continue to teach. Not only was she able to finish the school year, but the superintendent offered her a five-year contract, which was unheard of at the time. Three months later, Wavie and Laurence were married in the St. George Temple.

Before the five-year contract was up, the Petersons had had their first baby and had moved to Salt Lake, Ogden, and then to Milford, where Laurence was in partnership in a dairy. In late January 1937, the Petersons went to Kanarraville, Utah, to visit Wavie's father, who was in the hospital with lung cancer. While there, Wavie went into labor and went to the nearest hospital, which was in Cedar City, Utah. Pat was born on 3 February. Laurence was already in the hospital because he had broken several ribs in a skiing accident the day before, so the nurses brought Pat over for him to see. "I knew we had an angel," says Laurence of the first time he saw her.[2]

Wavie's father, John H. Williams, who was also in the same hospital, was able to see Pat but died six days after she was born. To compound the tragedy, Wavie's mother, Susannah, caught cold at John's burial, which took place during a snowstorm, and died a month later from pneumonia. Though Pat never knew her maternal grandparents, she learned the family stories from her mother. One of everyone's favorites was how Wavie got her name.

John and Susannah Williams raised their ten children in Kanarraville, Utah, where John worked as a sheep rancher. As the eighth of ten children, Wavie went nine months without a name while her parents, who had used up their favorite names on the other girls, tried to think of a name. One spring day, John and Susannah went to visit one of their sheepherders on Kanarra Mountain. While she was waiting, Susannah started reading a novel in the herder's wagon titled *Wavie the Sea Waif*. When the Williamses got home, Susannah suggested they name their baby daughter Wavie. They did, but Wavie remembers that "it caused me embarrassment when I was growing up."[3]

Pat's Latter-day Saint heritage on this line goes back to one of Susannah's ancestors, Shadrach Roundy, who learned of the gospel from the Prophet Joseph Smith during the winter of 1830–31. He and his family were baptized in 1831. He remained one of Joseph's dearest and most trusted friends throughout the life of the Prophet and even served as Joseph's bodyguard in Nauvoo. At nearly sixty years of age, Shadrach was the oldest member of the first pioneer company to arrive in the Salt Lake Valley. He crossed the plains five times helping immigrants come to Zion.

The only grandmother Pat ever knew was Laurence's mother, Annie. Pat loved this woman with whom she would eventually have so much in common. Annie loved children and Primary, where she served all of her life. And Annie was a skillful seamstress, as is Pat. Annie also had leadership skills, as Pat does; Annie put her skills to use in 1933 when she passed the state examination to become the juvenile probation officer for the 5th District.

Annie, the daughter of Francis and Elizabeth (Staheli) Walker, grew up in Spring Valley, Nevada, where her father worked as a rancher. Though Latter-day Saints, the Walkers did not live near any other Saints. Annie was fourteen when the family moved to Hinckley, Utah, after the death of Annie's brother and sister from diphtheria. It was here that Annie, who was then teaching school, met Alma Peterson, a returned missionary from England. They married and Alma took work as a miner in Eureka, a rip-roaring mining town where this Latter-day Saint family remained in the minority. It was here that Pat's father, Laurence, was born.

In spite of the boisterous lifestyle of most townspeople, the Petersons remained faithful in the Church. Kind-hearted Annie always kept homemade bread and vegetable soup ready to feed the many hungry strangers who came to her door. During the Depression years, hoboes commonly made a secret mark on homes where they could get a meal, and the Peterson house had such a mark.

After thirteen years in Eureka, Alma and Annie moved their family to Provo, Utah. In all, Pat grew up knowing of her Latter-day Saint pioneer ancestors and looking to them as examples.

A Self-Reliant Childhood

Laurence and Wavie lived in Provo with their four children until Pat was eight, and then the family moved to Hawaii for a change of job and in the spirit of adventure. Living in a small home in Kailua on the island of Oahu, the Petersons enjoyed the beauties of the area and a humble lifestyle while Laurence worked in the dairy business. Pat's summer days were filled with daily ocean swims and running barefoot in the sand. "At dawn, my friend would scratch on my screen and we would run about a block to the beach," says Pat. "We wanted to be the first there and search for treasures. Often we found glass balls that had come across the ocean from the nets of

Japanese fishermen and sometimes a beautiful shell. My father taught me about spear fishing, coral, and pulling weeds. My mother taught me the names of flowers and trees, and we wove mats from leaves. I remember my father's kind and gentle but firm ways. My mother instilled self-reliance in me by allowing me to be responsible for myself and not always fixing my mistakes."[4]

Laurence remembers Pat's spirituality as a child. "There is nothing better for a father than to hear his children pray and then tuck them into bed," he says. "When Pat prayed, she talked to her Heavenly Father, for she was very close to him."[5]

While in Hawaii, Laurence helped organize a small branch Sunday School in Kailua, and nine-year-old Pat played the pump organ. "My parents expected me to do hard things," says Pat. "I learned from that experience that I was needed. Now it reminds me how important it is for children to know they are needed and that they can be a helpful part of the Church."[6]

Laurence and Wavie moved from Hawaii to Glendale, California, when Pat was fourteen years old. Immediately, Pat realized that she needed different clothes from the casual ones she had worn in Hawaii. She took a sewing class in ninth grade, and then, drawing upon her own resources, she began making her own clothes, discovering in the process that she had a gift for sewing. "I can remember admiring her ability to design a dress and sew it up in one night," says Pat's sister, Laurelee.[7]

During her junior high school and high school years, Pat became part of a close group of Latter-day Saint youth in the La Canada Ward in the Glendale stake. Here, her testimony blossomed. At seventeen, Pat and her friends attended a series of firesides held on three consecutive Sundays. The speaker talked to the youth about the joys of building a relationship with the Savior. He suggested that each time they heard the school bell ring, they say a silent prayer and thank Heavenly Father for their blessings. He told them that they could also pray for a friend at the same time. "That sounded wonderful to me," says Pat. "I decided to try. . . . It was awkward at first, but soon I found myself thinking about my Heavenly Father and Savior, not only when the bell rang but many times during the day. . . . I loved him so much. My faith had increased, and I was happy."[8]

Pat's brother David remembers these years. "Keeping the gospel standards as a teenager was a great strength to Pat, and it was the way she brought joy and happiness into her life," he says. "I witnessed this in her face and in her actions on a daily basis during those years."[9]

Focus amid Change

The next ten years of Pat's life took her from being a high school senior to being a busy mother of a large family. These were years of rapid change and growth for her personally, and she met them with simple faith, optimism, and hard work. "There is nothing more profound and deep than a simple faith," says Pat. "My faith is the foundation of my life. Maybe it's simple, but that simpleness runs deep and is so strong that it guides me, protects me, and blesses me."[10]

Pat's goal was to attend Brigham Young University in Provo, Utah, and she worked at a dentist's office on Saturdays and summers during high school to earn the money for college. In the fall of 1955, Pat started her freshman year at BYU. During orientation, a senior basketball player, Ed J. Pinegar, gave a speech about the honor code. Pat, who was wearing a yellow sweater and a brown skirt, was sitting on the front row. They didn't even talk to each other that day, but Ed knew he wanted to find out who she was. For the next two nights, Ed visited the girls' dormitories asking if anyone knew a girl who had worn a yellow sweater and a brown skirt to orientation. He couldn't find her. A few days later, Ed was leaving basketball practice when he passed Pat, who was coming to try out for the Cougarettes, BYU's drill team. He stopped her and immediately asked her for a date. Six months later, on March 28, 1956, they were married in the Salt Lake Temple. "I'll never forget the love I felt for Pat that day in the temple as we became eternal companions," says Ed.[11]

During their first year of married life, Ed attended his last quarter of school. Pat, who had worked part-time during high school as a dental assistant, found a job with a Provo dentist. On the first day of work, however, she was so afflicted with morning sickness that the dentist decided she had better not keep her job. In June 1956, Ed graduated from college and went to work for Geneva Steel near Provo. Pat was sick much of the nine months of her pregnancy, but a healthy baby girl, Karie, was born in January 1957. Pat began what was to become the joy of her life—mothering.

After a year with Geneva Steel, Ed was accepted at dental school at the University of Southern California in Los Angeles, and the young Pinegar family moved. Steven was born in December of 1957, only eleven months after Karie, accelerating Pat's challenges as a new mother. Three years later, in late 1960, daughter Kelly was born.

These were hectic, challenging years for the Pinegars. Ed taught early-morning seminary, attended dental school, and worked for four hours in the evenings as a janitor. Meanwhile, Pat cared for their three children. Money was scarce during their student years, and Pat did ironing, mending, and telephoning for Deseret Industries at home. However, Pat's focus and joy were her children. For example, she created an ingenious play yard out of orange crates and boxes for the children. During the Pinegars' last year in California, Pat had her first opportunity to serve in a leadership position when she served as Relief Society president in the University of Southern California student ward.

When the Pinegars moved back to Provo in 1961 and Ed set up a dental practice, they thought they were there to stay. After one year of private practice, however, Ed was drafted into military service. As a captain in the army, he served as a dentist at Fort Lewis in Tacoma, Washington. Again Pat managed to make the adjustments of moving a family of young children and establishing a home in an area where they had no relatives. Drawing upon her optimistic nature and putting her trust in the Lord, Pat came to love living there. Opportunities for Church service abounded in their ward,

which was in the process of building a chapel, and soon Ed
was serving in the bishopric and Pat was serving as a counselor in the Relief Society. Kristin was born there in April 1963.
When Ed's military service was over, the Pinegars again moved
back to Provo in 1964 to be near family and friends. They
began building a home.

Putting Down Roots

All the years of moving and living in rented homes finally
came to an end for the Pinegars when, in 1965, they moved
into their new home in Oak Hills, a subdivision east of
Brigham Young University in Provo. Many other young families were also moving into the neighborhood at the time with
the idea of putting down roots. It was here that Pat came to a
turning point in her life as a young mother of four children,
including a new baby. "I love light, order, and calm feelings,"
says Pat. "I always wanted the floors to be clean to help contribute to that feeling of calm, but it was difficult to do with
toddlers. As a result, I vacuumed a lot. One day Ed came
home early and I was vacuuming. He gave me a big hug.
Then, joking with me, he said, 'I think I know what you'll be
doing in the eternities—you'll be the chief vacuumer.' I knew
he was kidding, but my life felt out of control. I thought, NO!
The next day I got a baby-sitter, took a stack of paper and my
scriptures, and went fasting to my parents' cabin in the mountains. I spent the day sorting out my life and taking control. I
prayed, wrote pages of lists, and prioritized everything.
Returning to my Heavenly Father with Ed and our children
was top priority. The things that came next were those things
that would help me get there, such as scripture study, temple
attendance, family home evening, and teaching our children.
Cleaning the drawers in the bathroom fell to the bottom of my
list. Then, as an exercise in returning to faith and values, I
drew up a plan and overlaid my list on a calendar so things
would happen. This was a monumental time in my life. I went
home excited, because I knew where I wanted to go."[12]

As Pat shared her experience with Ed, he willingly went

through the same priority-setting exercise with Pat in relationship to their family life. "This was a wonderful turning point in our marriage," says Pat. "We talked weekly about our goals and attended the temple regularly, with a focus on each of our children."[13] This ability to prioritize her life still stands as one of Pat's greatest character traits and has helped her to be successful in her personal, family, and public life.

Four more children were born to the Pinegars during this time: Brett in 1967, Cory in 1969, Traci in 1972, and Tricia in 1974. The Pinegar family now totaled eight children—five girls and three boys.

For the twenty-eight years the Pinegars lived here, the lives of many of the families were intertwined in neighborhood, school, and Church activities, and the Pinegars became close friends with their neighbors. During this time, the Pinegars also bought a cabin on the shore of Bear Lake, Idaho, where they enjoyed family activities such as water skiing and swimming.

These were years of great growth for Pat, who developed her leadership skills through serving in the Church and her mothering ability through raising eight children. Pat served in many leadership positions, including serving as the ward Relief Society president for the second time, as Young Women adviser and then president, as stake Young Women adviser and counselor, and as both ward and stake Primary president. She also served on the PTA board and then as president. "Any kind of service helps prepare us," says Pat. "We simply do the best we can, never give up, sacrifice and dedicate ourselves, and humble ourselves to receive inspiration. I have a testimony of the blessings that come from expressing gratitude to our Heavenly Father [and] from acknowledging his hand in our lives. He magnifies our abilities when we thank him for answering our prayers and guiding us."[14]

Of course, family is among the things for which Pat is most grateful. Comments from Ed and some of the Pinegar children give an intimate view of these years of Pat's mothering.

Ed says, "Pat's mind was always on how to bless, how to

serve, how to nurture, how to help, and how to encourage her family."[15]

"My first memory of my mother is her tickling my back before bedtime, while singing to me," says Traci. "Being a mother and a homemaker is an honor, not a chore, for her. She magnified this calling to the fullest, and she never misses a chance to say that she loves us. It's wonderful!"[16]

Tricia, the youngest, says, "My mom and I are hugging partners. Whenever I need a hug, she is always there. I also remember my mom waiting at the mailbox for me when I came home from school. It was comforting to see her waiting for me as the bus came down our street. My mom taught us how to work. We became self-reliant. Seventh grade was the year we learned to do our own wash. I also remember waking up at seven to pull weeds in the garden. In high school, I played sports. My mom would come to all of my basketball games. At first she would hold up three of her fingers to remind me to shoot 3-pointers. Then we got the saying WOW, meaning 'woman of worth,' so she would hold up three fingers on each side of her face and open her mouth in an O shape. The WOW sign reminded me to play my hardest. After she did the WOW sign, she would flip her hands upside down, spelling MOM."[17]

Steven says, "I know my mom would do anything for my welfare and benefit. At various times in my life, my mother fasted once a week specifically for me. Now I know what a sacrifice that was, but then it showed me her love, and it gave me the strength to keep the commandments."[18]

Family home evening was an important part of the Pinegar family life. But both Ed and Pat acknowledge that family home evening with eight children wasn't always easy. Daughter Kelly remembers one family home evening when the kids didn't pay attention. "We kept saying, 'Isn't the lesson over yet?' or 'I've got homework,' or 'What's for treats?' Well, we did the unpardonable—we made Mom cry. We said we were sorry, but we didn't know what to do. Mom was frustrated, but she never gave up on us. We kept having family home evening every Monday, and today we feel like we are a forever family."[19]

Brett remembers how his mother helped him build a robot. "As a child I was very interested in computers, robots, chemistry, astronomy," says Brett. "Most of my siblings were less interested in science and more interested in athletics. Mom regularly spent individual time with each of us. I remember being about seven or eight and wanting to build a robot. I told her what I wanted the robot to do, and we decided the best thing was to build a robot costume that I could wear. We cut, colored, and glued, and in no time we had created a great robot. I am so grateful for her desire to spend time with us doing whatever we children wanted to do."[20]

Missions and Memories

In 1985, Ed was called to serve for three years as the president of the England London South Mission. Oldest daughter Karie remembers when her father received the call. "There was not a complaint," says Karie. "There was no talk about hating to leave home, children, or grandchildren. There was only talk about the great opportunity to serve the Lord."[21]

The Pinegars took their four children who were still living at home. Kristi stayed in England with her parents for the summer and returned to Brigham Young University in the fall. Cory returned to Provo to finish his senior year in high school. "Serving in England was the beginning of my love and respect for missionaries," says Pat. "During those three years, our whole focus was on service, the Savior, and blessing people's lives. That is the real joy of missionary work."[22]

More than five hundred missionaries served between 1985 and 1988 with the Pinegars. Ed observed Pat's growth during these years. "We used to say that we must be exactly and immediately obedient to our leaders," he says, "and we both learned to follow the Brethren during these years."[23]

In September 1986, Cory went back to Provo. On the night of 17 October 1986, he was in a car accident and did not have his seat belt on. A serious head injury left him in a coma.

The Pinegars came home immediately, but Cory died a few days later without regaining consciousness. "I was grateful he was alive when I came home," says Pat. "His hand was warm as I held it."[24]

Daughter Kristi and Pat's sister, Laurelee, remember that time. "My mother had to fly home from England all alone because my dad couldn't come until the next day," says Kristi. "I think that would have been the longest plane ride in the world."[25]

Laurelee says, "When Cory died, I couldn't believe how strong Pat seemed. She said she was sure that as soon as Ed arrived, with his mighty faith, he would give Cory a blessing and he would get well, . . . but when she saw Cory, she knew that it was not to be. After the funeral she said that she could physically feel the love of the people who came bearing them up and supporting them. She said that they used to pray for the safety of their friends and relatives, but after Cory's death they realized that safety wasn't the most important thing. Now she prays for the righteousness of friends and relatives."[26]

Some wondered if the Pinegars would go back to London and finish their mission, but there was never a doubt in their own minds that they would continue to serve. "They were blessed with a peace that came from their faith," says Karie.[27]

As time passed, Pat shared what she had learned from this painful experience with others by her usual method—teaching by analogy. When you get into a car, "don't ever forget to put that seat belt on,'" she says. "When you click it on, think, 'Did I buckle up with prayer today? Did I read the scriptures today? Did I bless someone else?' If they would just think of those three things, they would be safer."[28]

In 1988, as Ed was finishing his service as mission president, he received a call to serve as the president of the Missionary Training Center (MTC) in Provo, Utah, immediately after he finished in England. "It was the best of all worlds," says Pat. "We could live at home, be with our family and friends, and still work with the missionaries."[29] Pat's role as wife of the MTC president was a joy to her. With her husband, Pat spoke weekly to every group of incoming missionaries and outgoing missionaries. She also worked closely with the sister missionaries in their Sunday meetings and had wonderful opportunities to visit one-on-one with the senior sisters.

Pat wanted to help the missionaries learn to love the scriptures, so she challenged them to read the scriptures daily and look for a spiritual principle that they could apply in their lives that day. Pat did the same thing. "Every day I posted a card outside my office door that had a scripture and a personal application of that scripture," says Pat. "It's crucial that we learn how the scriptures can help, strengthen, and guide us."[30]

More than thirty-five thousand missionaries passed through the MTC during the two years the Pinegars served there. A few months after the Pinegars finished their service at the MTC, Pat's mother died. "It was difficult for me to watch my mother slip away," she says. "My mother was a powerful influence in my life of beauty and creativity."

A Willingness to Serve

Pat loves spending time with children and grandchildren. "We really plan big events for grandchildren when we get together and have established some traditions besides Thanksgiving and Christmas. In the autumn, when the leaves are at their most beautiful, we go up into the canyon and cook breakfast outdoors. In the summer, we get everyone together at least once at Bear Lake. I have such a delightful time planning the activities. We mix glycerin in soap and blow giant bubbles, and then we play with the bubbles. We paint our shadows, swim, and talk."[31]

Daughter Traci comments on Pat's talents and perseverance: "My mom has always been a hard worker," says Traci. "Even while taking care of eight children, she managed her time so she could take up quilting as a hobby. Quilting taught my mom how to accomplish large tasks by taking one small step a time. One summer at Bear Lake, Mom was cleaning up the beach to make it look nice. I went down to help her. During the conversation, she brought up the notion that if she wanted she could change the shape of the whole beach with a shovel and a wheelbarrow. I said, 'There is no way! The beach is huge.' She simply replied, 'I know I can do it, because I'm a quilter.'"[32]

The Pinegars also have a yearly honor dinner on Cory's birthday. They serve his favorite foods and remember the good things he taught them.

In October 1991, Pat was called to serve on the Primary general board. "My life has been focused on being a wife and a mother of eight children," she says. "I have spent my time at home with my family and doing some community service like PTA. Going on a mission really expanded my vision of the worldwide church and helped me see the earth as the home of Heavenly Father's children. All of this helped prepare me to serve on the Primary board. During this short six months, I experienced the art of committee work, sharing ideas, and strong feelings when working together to come to a happy consensus. I also had the opportunity to visit some inner-city Primaries and do some training."[33] As part of their board responsibilities, board members taught Primary in their own wards. Pat taught a Star A class.

On March 3, 1992, only six months after her call to the general board, Pat was called to serve in the Young Women general presidency as a counselor to Janette C. Hales. "Pat's desire to pattern her life after the Savior became evident to me when I served as her counselor in our ward Relief Society presidency in 1970," says Janette. "I don't ever remember her being involved in discussions about the personal lives of the sisters in our ward. She simply assessed needs and gave service."[34]

As a member of the Young Women presidency, Pat also served with first counselor Virginia Pearce. Of her experience in the Young Women presidency, Pat says, "I experienced real growth as our presidency discussed and shared around the round table in the Young Women office. Virginia was so supportive. I did a great deal of uncomfortable stretching and growing."[35]

One of Pat's main responsibilities was to arrange leadership training for Young Women leaders throughout the world. She worked with regional representatives and area presiden-

cies to set up the training. She traveled to the Philippines and
in the United States and Canada. "It was wonderful to go out
and meet with people who are actually doing the work," she
says. "My thinking expanded, and I began to think of Young
Women worldwide. I became aware of the challenges the
young women are facing throughout the world. I firmly
believe that the gospel of Jesus Christ is the answer to those
challenges."[36]

The year 1994 brought many changes with it. The
Pinegars moved from their beloved Oak Hills neighborhood
into a new home also in Provo. Pat and Ed invited Pat's father
to live with them so he would not be alone. He did, and it has
been an opportunity for the Pinegars to be with him more
often and enjoy his company. "Pat has a tremendous commitment to family," says Janette Hales Beckham. "She regularly
includes Ed's mother, who has been a widow since his childhood, in their family gatherings. She cared for her own mother
until her mother's death, and she made a place for her father
to live with them. The Pinegar home is a place of love, fun,
and hospitality, along with a healthy amount of hard work and
responsibility."[37]

Ninth General President

At the October 1994 general conference, Pat was sus-
tained as Primary general president, with Anne Goalen
Wirthlin as her first counselor and Susan Carol Lilywhite
Warner as her second counselor.

"How grateful I am for the principle of presidency, and
for Sister Anne Wirthlin and Sister Susan Warner," says Pat. "In
the multitude of counselors there is safety' (Proverbs 11:14). I
love these women; we will stand together in unity as we support our priesthood leaders in helping families and Primaries
to teach and strengthen children."[38]

Sister Warner, who served as Pat's counselor in a stake
Primary presidency almost twenty years ago, says, "I learned
when I served with Pat before, and it has been reaffirmed as I
work closely with her now, that she is one who consistently

evaluates her priorities and eliminates her involvement in activities that do not support her immediate or long-range goals. Her example has given others courage to move ahead and leave the regrets of the past behind. She is open and eager to hear the views of others. Though she listens and carefully weighs issues and alternatives, she has faith that she will be guided and receive divine direction. The scriptural phrase that defines her leadership style is 'Confidence that has waxed strong in the Lord.' She reminds us all that this is the Lord's church and he has a plan we must discover."[39]

Pat feels that mothering has been the greatest preparation for her calling as Primary president. "Mothering has been and still is the most important part of my life," says Pat. "I always wanted to be a mother, and Ed and I were delighted as each baby was born. It was wonderful to watch each child grow up over the years and to see how different they each are. I love them so dearly. Each one has a special strength within, and I have learned so much from them. They continue to bless my life."[40]

Ed has seen a difference in Pat since she began serving in the Primary. "When Pat starts talking about Primary, she becomes slightly transformed," he says. "Each of us is endowed with the mantle of authority for our calling, and I can see it on Pat."[41]

Talking about Primary and children comes easily for Pat. "I am so excited about representing and speaking for children," she says. "I will do anything I can in their behalf. Children have so many Christlike attributes, and they are so pure. Between the ages of one and eight years old, they have such an ability to learn and to retain information that will stay with them throughout their lives. If we want children to be morally clean, make wise choices, and become responsible adults, we need to lay a gospel foundation when they are very young and excited about learning. That is the prime time to teach them."[42]

The year 1995 began with a new simplified Primary program conceived and put into place before Pat was called as president. However, it was her job to implement the program.

Three lesson manuals replaced eleven. Children were still divided by individual age, but one manual was to be used for more than one age group. Each lesson in the new manuals contains ideas on how to adapt it for different age levels. To support the new curriculum and give identity to the children in the worldwide Church, children will be identified as Sunbeams from eighteen months to three years of age; as CTRs from four to seven years old; and as Valiants from ages eight to twelve. The Achievement Days program has been expanded to include 8-year-old girls. Eight-year-old boys will continue the Scouting program where it is approved.

As part of her calling as Primary general president, Pat also serves on the National Advisory Council of the Boy Scouts of America and the National Cub Scout Council of the Boy Scouts of America.

"Come unto Christ"

Pat is well aware of children throughout the world who are suffering for any number of reasons. "I think Primary can help children who are hurting," she says. "In Isaiah 11:6 it says that during the millennium 'the wolf also shall dwell with the lamb . . . and a little child shall lead them.' It goes on to say in verse nine that 'they shall not hurt nor destroy . . . for the earth shall be full of the knowledge of the Lord.' Our homes and our Primary classrooms can be places of peace, safety, growth, and love for our children. They can be 'full of the knowledge of the Lord.' In Primaries around the world, I would encourage teachers to share their feelings of Jesus with the children, to 'talk of Christ, to rejoice in Christ' (2 Nephi 25:26). I feel strongly that this must be our focus, our quest; to fill each child with stories, songs, examples of the Savior. I want them to trust Him and love Him enough that they will choose to follow Him. Children will have a desire to choose to obey if they really understand in their hearts how much Heavenly Father and Jesus Christ love them. They will want to 'come unto Christ.'"[43]

Patricia Peterson Pinegar also desires to "come unto

Christ." Her favorite scripture is found in Proverbs 3:5–6: 'Trust in the Lord with all thine heart; and lean not to your own understanding. In all thy ways acknowledge him, and he shall direct thy paths." Pat has placed her trust in the Lord throughout her life. Her faith, optimism, and work ethic have given her the ability to raise eight children, the courage to carry on after the death of a child, and the skills to serve as a leader in the Church. She knows the source of the light in her life. It is the Savior, Jesus Christ, and, like the tenacious sunflower that turns to the sun for its light and strength, she turns to the Savior for hers.

Appendix

Primary Time Line

1830	The Church of Jesus Christ of Latter-day Saints is organized on April 6 in Fayette, New York
1830–44	Joseph Smith serves as first prophet and president of the restored church
1844–77	Brigham Young presides over the Church
1861–65	U.S. Civil War
1866–80	Eliza R. Snow leads all women's auxiliaries, including Primary
1877–87	John Taylor presides over the Church
1878	First ward Primary is organized in Farmington, Utah, by Aurelia Spencer Rogers; other ward Primaries soon follow
1880	Separate presidencies for Primary, YLMIA, and Relief Society are organized by President John Taylor
1880–1925	LOUIE BOUTON FELT serves as first Primary general president
1881	Eliza R. Snow prepares first Primary songbook
1887–98	Wilford Woodruff presides over the Church
1893	Salt Lake Temple is dedicated
1898–1901	Lorenzo Snow is fifth president of the Church

1901–18	Joseph F. Smith is sixth president of the Church
1902	First issue of the *Children's Friend* is published; May Anderson is appointed editor, serves as editor for 38 years
1905	*The Primary Songbook* is published
1913	Church begins sponsoring Scouting program
1913	Primary establishes children's unit at Groves LDS Hospital
1914–18	World War I
1918–45	Heber J. Grant is seventh president of the Church
1922	Convalescent home for children is opened
1925–39	MAY ANDERSON serves as second general president of the Primary
1928	Primary Jubilee
1929	Religion classes are discontinued; Primary classes incorporate more religious instruction
1939–45	World War II
1940	Primary seal is designed; Primary colors are selected
1940–43	MAY GREEN HINCKLEY is third general president of the Primary
1943–51	ADELE CANNON HOWELLS is fourth general president of the Primary
1945–51	George Albert Smith is eighth president of the Church
1946	*Children's Friend of the Air,* a series of fifteen-minute radio programs for children, is broadcast
1947	For centennial of pioneers' arrival in Salt Lake Valley, Primary children present commemorative program throughout Church
1948	*Junior Council,* a television series of half-hour programs for children, is broadcast
1950–53	Korean War

1951	*The Children Sing* is published
1951–70	David O. McKay is ninth president of the Church
1951–74	LaVern Watts Parmley serves as fifth general president of the Primary
1952	Fiftieth anniversary of *Children's Friend*
1952	Primary Children's Hospital is dedicated
1953	Cub Scout program and Scouting for eleven-year-old boys are reassigned to be supervised by Primary
1957	Song "I Am a Child of God" is introduced at Primary conference
1965–73	Vietnam War
1970	*Sing with Me* is published
1970–72	Joseph Fielding Smith is tenth president of the Church
1971	*Children's Friend* is renamed *The Friend*
1972–73	Harold B. Lee serves as eleventh president of the Church
1973–85	Spencer W. Kimball is twelfth president of the Church
1974	Church donates medical facilities, including Primary Children's Medical Center, to nonprofit organization; the center continues in operation, managed by Intermountain Health Care
1974–80	Naomi Maxfield Shumway serves as sixth general president of the Primary
1975	Last Primary conference is held
1975	Penny Parade is replaced with Primary Birthday Pennies
1978	Centennial of Primary
1978	Revelation on priesthood
1980	Consolidated meeting schedule begins; Primary meets on Sundays instead of weekdays

1980	Sesquicentennial of the Church
1980–88	DWAN JACOBSEN YOUNG is seventh general president of the Primary
1985–94	Ezra Taft Benson is thirteenth president of the Church
1988	Primary, Young Women, and Relief Society offices move into remodeled Relief Society Building
1988–94	MICHAELENE PACKER GRASSLI is eighth general president of the Primary
1989	*Children's Songbook* is published
1994–	PATRICIA PETERSON PINEGAR is ninth general president of the Primary
1994	Satellite broadcast, "Focus on Children," is presented
1994	*Teach the Child* video is released
1994–95	Howard William Hunter is fourteenth president of the Church
1995–	Gordon Bitner Hinckley is fifteenth president of the Church
1995	New lesson manuals are published (three instead of eleven); three age groups classified

Notes

Introduction

1. Junius F. Wells, quoted in Kate B. Carter, *Our Pioneer Heritage* (Salt Lake City: Daughters of Utah Pioneers, 1972), 134–35.

2. Brigham Young, in *Journal of Discourses,* 19:43; quoted in Conrad A. Harward, "A History of the Growth and Development of the Primary Association of the LDS Church from 1878 to 1928" (master's thesis, Brigham Young University, 1976), 12.

3. Aurelia S. Rogers, *Life Sketches of Orson Spencer and Others, and History of Primary Work* (Salt Lake City: George Q. Cannon and Sons Co., 1898), 205–6.

4. Ibid., 208.

5. Ibid., 209.

6. Ibid., 212.

7. *Woman's Exponent* 7 (1 September 1878):54; quoted in Carol Cornwall Madsen and Susan Staker Oman, *Sisters and Little Saints: One Hundred Years of Primary* (Salt Lake City: Deseret Book Co., 1978), 7.

8. Primary minutes, Farmington Ward, Davis Stake, 1 (25 August 1878): 5, manuscript in Archives Division, Church Historical Department, The Church of Jesus Christ of Latter-day Saints, Salt Lake City; hereafter cited as Church Archives. Quoted in Susan Oman and Carol Madsen, "100 Years of Primary," *Ensign,* April 1978, 33.

Chapter One: Louie Bouton Felt

1. "Louie B. Felt," *Children's Friend,* October 1919, 407.

2. Ibid., 404.

3. Ibid., 406.

4. Adelaide U. Hardy, "Living for a Purpose," *Children's Friend,* December 1918, 474.

5. "Louie B. Felt," *Children's Friend,* October 1919, 408.

6. Augusta Joyce Crocheron, *Representative Women of Deseret* (Salt Lake City: J. C. Graham & Co., 1884), 58.

7. "Louie B. Felt," *Children's Friend,* October 1919, 409.

8. "Louie B. Felt," *Mormon Biographical Sketches Collection,* 1:11:8, Church Archives.

9. Ettie Felt Toronto, "History of Sarah Louise Bouton Felt: 'Louie Ma,'" 21 November 1963, unpublished family history in possession of Linda Lamborn.

10. "Louie B. Felt," *Mormon Biographical Sketches Collection,* 1:11:8.

11. "Louie B. Felt," *Children's Friend,* October 1919, 411.

12. Lillie T. Freeze, "A Bit of History," holograph, Lillie T. Freeze Papers, Church Archives.

13. Telephone interview with Bud Keysor, 29 September 1994.

14. Ibid.

15. Louie B. Felt, "Remarks at June 1908 Conference," *Children's Friend,* June 1908, 276.

16. May Anderson, "Primary Work of Yesterday and Today," *Children's Friend,* February 1933, 62.

17. "Louie B. Felt," *Children's Friend,* October 1919, 413.

18. Ibid.

19. Ibid.

20. Aurelia Spencer Rogers, *Life Sketches of Orson Spencer and Others, and History of Primary Work* (Salt Lake City: George Q. Cannon & Sons, 1898), 222–23.

21. *Children's Friend,* December 1918, 476.

22. Freeze, "A Bit of History."

23. Lillie T. Freeze, "Primary Work from 1880–1890," 2, holograph, Lillie T. Freeze Papers, Church Archives.

24. Louie Morris White, "Recalling the Past," 1928, typescript, Church Archives.

25. Minutes of the Primary General Board, 1889–1901, 3 October 1889, 3, Church Archives; quoted in Carol Cornwall Madsen and Susan Staker Oman, *Sisters and Little Saints: One Hundred Years of Primary* (Salt Lake City: Deseret Book Co., 1979), 36.

26. Primary minutes, 4; quoted in Madsen and Oman, *Sisters and Little Saints,* 37.

27. Conrad A. Harward, "A History of the Growth and Development of

the Primary Association of the LDS Church from 1878 to 1928" (master's thesis, Brigham Young University, 1976), 190.

28. May Anderson, "The Spirit of Primary," *Children's Friend*, October 1934, 349.

29. Ibid.

30. Allan Dean Payne, "The Mormon Response to Early Progressive Education, 1892–1920" (Ph.D. dissertation, University of Utah, 1977).

31. Freeze, "Primary Work from 1880–1890."

32. *Woman's Exponent*, 1 January 1901, 69–70.

33. Madsen and Oman, *Sisters and Little Saints*, 57.

34. Harward, "A History of the Growth and Development of the Primary Association," 79.

35. Minutes of the Primary General Board, 23 February 1922, 122; quoted in Harward, "A History of the Growth and Development of the Primary Association," 245.

36. "Report of Soldiers' Supplies," *Children's Friend*, April 1918, 187.

37. Harward, "A History of the Growth and Development of the Primary Association," 194–96.

38. Marion Belnap Kerr, "A Tribute to Louie B. Felt," *Children's Friend*, March 1928, 100.

39. "Louie B. Felt: A Tribute," *Children's Friend*, November 1925, 424.

40. Kerr, "A Tribute to Louie B. Felt," 101.

Chapter Two: May Anderson

1. "The New Presidency," *Children's Friend*, January 1926, 22.

2. "Mary and May," *Children's Friend*, October 1919, 419.

3. Ibid., 419.

4. Ibid.

5. "The New Presidency," 22.

6. "We Like Her Because She Helps Us Be Good," *Children's Friend*, April 1940, 150.

7. Telephone interview with Bud Keysor, 29 September 1994.

8. "The Children's Friend," *Children's Friend*, January 1922, 54.

9. See Adelaide U. Hardy, "The Children's Friend," *Children's Friend*, June 1918, 232.

10. *Children's Friend*, January 1912, 28.

11. "May Anderson, A Friend of Children," *Children's Friend*, April 1940, 152.

12. Frances Grant Bennett, *Glimpses of a Mormon Family* (Salt Lake City: Deseret Book Co., 1968), 176–77.

13. Ibid., 175–77.

14. Milton Lynn Bennion, *Mormonism and Education* (Salt Lake City: Department of Education, The Church of Jesus Christ of Latter-day Saints, 1939), 242.

15. Bennion, *Mormonism and Education,* 244; Marion B. Kerr, "The Primary Association Yesterday and Today," *Improvement Era,* April 1935, 272.

16. Bennion, *Mormonism and Education,* 244–45.

17. Carol Cornwall Madsen and Susan Staker Oman, *Sisters and Little Saints: One Hundred Years of Primary* (Salt Lake City: Deseret Book Co., 1979), 83–84.

18. Ibid., 86–88.

19. Ibid., 75–76.

20. "The Primary Association—Sixty Years Ago and Today," *Children's Friend,* July 1938, 275.

21. "In Tribute to May Anderson," *Children's Friend,* August 1946, 349.

22. May Anderson, "A Testimony," *Children's Friend,* April 1940, 150.

23. Madsen and Oman, *Sisters and Little Saints,* 81.

24. Ibid., 94.

25. "In Tribute to May Anderson," 349.

Chapter Three: May Green Hinckley

1. *The Guide,* June 1939.

2. Interview with President Gordon B. Hinckley, 13 October 1993.

3. Ibid.

4. Interview with Ramona H. Sullivan, 15 May 1993.

5. Interview with Joan W. Peterson, 15 May 1993.

6. Scrapbook of Bryant S. Hinckley family, 1932, in possession of Joan W. Peterson.

7. Interview with Carol H. Cannon, 15 May 1993.

8. Ibid.

9. Lucile H. Laxman, quoted in *Autobiography of Bryant S. Hinckley,* ed. Ruth Hinckley Willes and Joseph S. Willes (n.p.: Ruth Hinckley Willes, 1971), appendix 1; copy in Church Archives.

10. Interview with Ramona H. Sullivan, 15 May 1993.

11. Interview with President Gordon B. Hinckley, 13 October 1993.

12. Interview with Ramona H. Sullivan, 15 May 1993.

13. Ibid.

14. Ibid.

15. Ibid.

16. *Autobiography of Bryant S. Hinckley,* ed. Willes and Willes, 45.

17. Interview with President Gordon B. Hinckley, 13 October 1993.

18. Interview with Carol H. Cannon, 15 May 1993.

19. Interview with Ramona H. Sullivan, 15 May 1993.

20. Ibid.

21. *Autobiography of Bryant S. Hinckley,* ed. Willes and Willes, 37, 39–40.

22. Ibid., 39.

23. Ibid., 47.

24. Ibid.

25. Interview with Ramona H. Sullivan, 15 May 1993.

26. *The Guide,* June 1939.

27. "English-Born Leader Guides Destiny of 102,000 Children," *Church News,* 4 April 1964, 20.

28. *The Autobiography of Bryant S. Hinckley,* ed. Willes and Willes, 45.

29. LaVern Watts Parmley Oral History, James Moyle Oral History Program, Church Archives, 44; hereafter referred to as Parmley Oral History.

30. *Children's Songbook,* 1989, 258.

31. Carol Cornwall Madsen and Susan Oman Staker, *Sisters and Little Saints: One Hundred Years of Primary* (Salt Lake City: Deseret Book Co., 1979), 102–3.

32. Madsen and Staker, *Sisters and Little Saints,* 103.

33. Ibid., 105.

34. Interview with Ramona H. Sullivan, 15 May 1993.

35. Interview with Barbara H. Moench, 15 May 1993.

36. Primary notebook of May Green Hinckley, in possession of Joan W. Peterson.

37. Interview with President Gordon B. Hinckley, 13 October 1993.

38. Ibid.

39. Ibid.

40. Interview with Ramona H. Sullivan, 15 May 1993.

Chapter Four: Adele Cannon Howells

1. Adele Cannon Howells diary, 1 May 1946, microfilm, Church Archives.

2. Beatrice Cannon Evans and Janath Russell Cannon, eds., *Cannon Family Historical Treasury* (Salt Lake City: Cannon Family Association, 1987), 34.

3. Dessie Grant Boyle, "Adele Cannon Howells," in "Illustrated History of the Primary," 1, microfilm, Church Archives.

4. Ibid.

5. Ibid., 1–2.

6. Ibid., 2.

7. "Adele Cannon Howells—A Beloved Leader," *Children's Friend,*
August 1953, 357.

8. Ibid., 358.

9. Telephone interview with Barbara H. Moench, 12 May 1994.

10. Boyle, "Adele Cannon Howells," 5.

11. Ibid., 7.

12. Telephone interview with Barbara H. Moench, 12 May 1994.

13. Ibid.

14. Ibid.

15. Telephone interview with Barbara H. Moench, 27 May 1994.

16. Telephone interview with Barbara H. Moench, 12 May 1994.

17. Ibid.

18. Adele Cannon Howells diary, 12 March 1940, 15 March 1941, and
5 August 1941.

19. Telephone interview with Barbara H. Moench, 12 May 1994.

20. Adele Cannon Howells diary, 29 April 1945 and 2 February 1946.

21. Ibid., 3 June 1940.

22. Carol Cornwall Madsen and Susan Staker Oman, *Sisters and Little
Saints: One Hundred Years of Primary* (Salt Lake City: Deseret Book Co.,
1979), 106–7.

23. *Autobiography of Bryant S. Hinckley,* ed. Ruth Hinckley Willes and
Joseph S. Willes (n.p.: Ruth Hinckley Willes, 1971), 45; copy in Church
Archives.

24. Adele Cannon Howells diary, 3 May 1943.

25. Ibid., 19 July 1943 and 15 May 1945.

26. Ibid., 19 July 1943.

27. See Conrad A. Harward, "A History of the Growth and Development
of the Primary Association of the LDS Church from 1878 to 1928" (master's
thesis, Brigham Young University, 1976), 215–16.

28. "Primary, 1940–1974," in *Encyclopedia of Mormonism,* ed. Daniel H.
Ludlow (New York: Macmillan Publishing Co., 1992), 3:1146–50.

29. Adele Cannon Howells diary, 20 July 1945.

30. Madsen and Oman, *Sisters and Little Saints,* 120.

31. Adele Cannon Howells diary, 31 March, 29 September, and
15 October 1944; 19 May 1944.

32. Telephone interview with Lorin L. Moench, 26 May 1994.

33. Adele Cannon Howells diary, 24 January 1943 and 15 October 1946.

34. Madsen and Staker, *Sisters and Little Saints,* 130.

35. "Adele Cannon Howells—A Beloved Leader," *Children's Friend,*
August 1953, 357.

36. Adele Cannon Howells diary, 30 March 1944.

37. Ibid., 31 January 1946 and 26 July 1950.
38. Telephone interview with Lorin L. Moench, 25 May 1994.
39. Adele Cannon Howells diary, 4 February 1944.
40. Telephone interview with Barbara H. Moench, 12 May 1994.
41. Boyle, "Adele Cannon Howells," 7.

Chapter Five: LaVern Watts Parmley

1. Dell Van Orden, "The Lord Was Preparing Me to Be a Leader of Boys," *Church News,* 30 November 1968, 11.
2. Martha Jane Park Pexton Hulse, "William and Jane Duncan Park," typescript in possession of June Watts Jensen.
3. Martha Jane Park Pexton Hulse, "History of Jane Ann Ellison Park," typescript in possession of June Watts Jensen.
4. LaVern Watts Parmley, as quoted by Thomas J. Parmley.
5. Telephone interview with Maurice L. Watts, 6 February 1993.
6. Richard Dahl, *BYU's Stan Watts: The Man and His Game* (Bountiful, Utah: Horizon Publishers, 1976), 16.
7. Thomas J. Parmley, untitled tribute to LaVern Watts Parmley, n.d., copy in possession of Janet Peterson.
8. Dahl, *BYU's Stan Watts,* 17.
9. Van Orden, "The Lord Was Preparing Me to Be a Leader of Boys," 11.
10. LaVern Watts Parmley Oral History, 1974, James Moyle Oral History Program, Church Archives, 1; hereafter referred to as Parmley Oral History.
11. LaVern Watts Parmley, interview by Richard W. Muir, 30 January 1972, transcription in possession of Janet Peterson.
12. Telephone interview with Stan Watts, 3 May 1993.
13. Parmley Oral History, 2.
14. LaVern Watts Parmley, interview by Richard W. Muir, 30 January 1972, transcription.
15. Dahl, *BYU's Stan Watts,* 24.
16. LaVern Watts Parmley, interview by Richard W. Muir, 30 January 1972, transcription.
17. Telephone interview with Maurice L. Watts, 6 February 1993.
18. Ibid.
19. LaVern Watts Parmley, interview by Richard W. Muir, 30 January 1972, transcription.
20. Van Orden, "The Lord Was Preparing Me to Be a Leader of Boys," 11.
21. Parmley Oral History, 10.
22. Ibid., 7.

23. Gerry Avant, "BSA Has 'Expert' on Council," *Church News,* 3 November 1973, 6.

24. Telephone interview with Frances Parmley Muir, 19 May 1993.

25. Telephone interview with Richard T. Parmley, 3 May 1993.

26. Telephone interview with William W. Parmley, 4 May 1993.

27. Telephone interview with Frances Parmley Muir, 19 May 1993.

28. Telephone interview with Thomas J. Parmley, 19 March 1993.

29. Telephone interview with Vickie Muir Stewart, 18 May 1993.

30. Telephone interview with Beryl Watts Neff, 23 April 1993.

31. Blessing of LaVern Watts Parmley, n.d., copy in possession of Janet Peterson.

32. Parmley Oral History, 14–15.

33. Ibid., 18.

34. Telephone interview with Frances Parmley Muir, 19 May 1993.

35. Telephone interview with Richard T. Parmley, 3 May 1993.

36. Telephone interview with William W. Parmley, 4 May 1993.

37. Parmley Oral History, 36.

38. Ibid., 10.

39. Telephone interview with Trilba J. Lindsay, 13 May 1993.

40. Ibid.

41. Interview with Dwan J. Young, 26 May 1993.

42. Parmley Oral History, 134.

43. Telephone interview with Vickie Muir Stewart, 18 May 1993.

44. Carol Cornwall Madsen and Susan Staker Oman, *Sisters and Little Saints: One Hundred Years of Primary* (Salt Lake City: Deseret Book Co., 1978), 144, 210–12.

45. Karen Lynn Davidson, *Our Latter-day Hymns: The Stories and the Messages* (Salt Lake City: Deseret Book Co., 1988), 301.

46. Madsen and Oman, *Sisters and Little Saints,* 152.

47. Parmley Oral History, 34.

48. Madsen and Oman, *Sisters and Little Saints,* 135–36.

49. Parmley Oral History, 21.

50. Ibid., 22.

51. Quoted in Kate B. Carter, *Our Pioneer Heritage* (Salt Lake City: Daughters of Utah Pioneers, 1972), 161–62.

52. Parmley Oral History, 76.

53. Ibid., 100.

54. Madsen and Oman, *Sisters and Little Saints,* 172.

55. Parmley Oral History, 33.

56. See *Encyclopedia of Mormonism,* ed. Daniel H. Ludlow (New York: Macmillan Publishing Co., 1992), 2:660.

57. Parmley Oral History, 108, 113.

58. Ibid., 110.

59. Telephone interview with June Watts Jensen, 6 February 1993.

60. Telephone interview with Maurice L. Watts, 6 February 1993.

61. Dwan J. Young, "A Tribute to LaVern W. Parmley," address given to Primary General Board, Salt Lake City, 14 November 1974; typescript in possession of Janet Peterson.

62. LaVern Watts Parmley, interview by Richard W. Muir, 31 January 1972, transcription.

63. Van Orden, "The Lord Was Preparing Me to Be a Leader of Boys," 11.

64. Parmley Oral History, 23.

65. Telephone interview with Vickie Muir Stewart, 18 May 1993.

66. Telephone interview with Trilba Lindsay, 13 May 1993.

67. Telephone interview with Frances Parmley Muir, 19 May 1993.

68. Parmley Oral History, 156.

69. Interview with Thomas J. Parmley, 19 March 1993.

70. Telephone interview with Frances Parmley Muir, 19 May 1993.

Chapter Six: Naomi Maxfield Shumway

1. Telephone interview with Dorthea C. Murdock, 24 January 1994.

2. Maxfield family history, in possession of A. Vard Maxfield.

3. Interview with Naomi M. Shumway, 17 February 1993.

4. Interview with Naomi M. Shumway, 17 February 1993.

5. Telephone interview with Leah M. Sims, 16 November 1993.

6. Interview with Naomi M. Shumway, 17 February 1993.

7. Ibid.

8. Telephone interview with Naomi M. Shumway, 2 November 1994.

9. Interview with Naomi M. Shumway, 17 February 1993.

10. Telephone interview with Roden G. Shumway, 4 January 1994.

11. Telephone interview with Naomi M. Shumway, 2 November 1994.

12. Interview with Jan S. Christensen, 28 October 1993.

13. Telephone interview with Roger G. Shumway, 12 January 1994.

14. Telephone interview with Dorthea C. Murdock, 24 January 1994.

15. Interview with Naomi M. Shumway, 17 February 1993.

16. Interview with Jan S. Christensen, 28 October 1993.

17. Telephone interview with Shari S. Oman, 3 November 1993.

18. Interview with Naomi M. Shumway, 17 February 1993.

19. Interview with Jan S. Christensen, 28 October 1993.

20. Telephone interview with Leah M. Sims, 16 November 1993.

21. Interview with Naomi M. Shumway, 17 February 1993.

22. Notes of Naomi M. Shumway, copy in possession of Janet Peterson.

23. Interview with Jan S. Christensen, 28 October 1993.

24. Interview with Naomi M. Shumway, 17 February 1993.

25. Telephone interview with Roden G. Shumway, 4 January 1994.

26. As quoted by Colleen B. Lemmon in a telephone interview with Janet Peterson, 16 February 1994.

27. Carol Cornwall Madsen and Susan Stake Oman, *Sisters and Little Saints: One Hundred Years of Primary* (Salt Lake City: Deseret Book Co., 1979), 183.

28. Telephone interview with Sara B. Paulsen, 14 January 1994.

29. Telephone interview with Trilba J. Lindsay, 29 January 1994.

30. Interview with Dwan J. Young, 26 May 1993.

31. Telephone interview with Colleen B. Lemmon, 16 February 1994.

32. Quoted in Ardeth G. Kapp Oral History, James H. Moyle Oral History Program, Church Archives, 104.

33. Telephone interview with Sara B. Paulsen, 14 January 1994.

34. "Dinner Climaxes Primary's Centennial," *Church News,* 26 August 1978, 6.

35. Gerry Avant, "Primary Will Reach Millions," *Church News,* 26 August 1978, 6.

36. Interview with Naomi M. Shumway, 17 February 1993.

37. Telephone interview with Colleen B. Lemmon, 16 February 1994.

38. Interview with Naomi M. Shumway, 17 February 1993.

39. Telephone interview with Janet C. Shumway, 9 November 1993.

40. Telephone interview with Roger G. Shumway, 12 January 1994.

41. Telephone interview with Janet C. Shumway, 9 November 1993.

42. Telephone interview with Shari S. Oman, 3 November 1993.

43. Interview with Naomi M. Shumway, 17 February 1993.

44. Telephone interview with Trilba J. Lindsay, 29 January 1994.

Chapter Seven: Dwan Jacobsen Young

1. Derin Lea Head, "Of Primary Concern," *This People,* August/September 1984, 54.

2. Telephone interview with Virginia B. Cannon, 5 January 1994.

3. Telephone interview with Dwan J. Young, 2 March 1994.

4. Telephone interview with Virginia B. Cannon, 5 January 1994.

5. Reuben Miller family history, in possession of Dwan J. Young.

6. Interview with Dwan J. Young, 26 May 1993.

7. Ibid.

8. Telephone interview with Alan Jacobsen, 1 March 1994.

9. Interview with Dwan J. Young, 26 May 1993.

10. Janet Peterson, "Dwan J. Young: Primarily Devoted to Children," *Ensign,* April 1986, 34.

11. Ibid.

12. Telephone interview with Dwan J. Young, 9 November 1994.

13. Interview with Vauna S. Jacobsen, 5 January 1994.

14. Interview with Dwan J. Young, 26 May 1993.

15. Dwan J. Young, "Prepare to Teach His Children," *Ensign,* November 1986, 3.

16. Peterson, "Dwan J. Young: Primarily Devoted to Children," 34.

17. Interview with Dwan J. Young, 26 May 1993.

18. Peterson, "Dwan J. Young: Primarily Devoted to Children," 34.

19. Ibid., 34–35.

20. Ibid., 35.

21. Ibid.

22. Ibid.

23. Ibid.

24. Telephone interview with Christine Y. Knudson, 18 January 1994.

25. Telephone interview with Paul Young, 22 March 1994.

26. Peterson, "Dwan J. Young: Primarily Devoted to Children," 34.

27. Interview with Dwan J. Young, 26 May 1993.

28. Ibid.

29. Ibid.

30. Peterson, "Dwan J. Young: Primarily Devoted to Children," 34.

31. Interview with Dwan J. Young, 26 May 1993.

32. Ibid.

33. "A Look at Primary on Its 105th Birthday: A Conversation with Dwan J. Young, General Primary President," *Ensign,* September 1983, 77.

34. Ibid.

35. "Young Women, Primary Offices Will Be Moved," *Ensign,* October 1984, 79.

36. Telephone interview with Virginia B. Cannon, 5 January 1994.

37. Written statement of Michaelene P. Grassli, 29 March 1994, in possession of Janet Peterson.

38. Interview with Dwan J. Young, 26 May 1993.

39. Telephone interview with Thomas Young, 15 March 1994.

40. Interview with Dwan J. Young, 26 May 1993.

41. "Primary, 1982: A Conversation with the General Primary Presidency," *Ensign,* January 1982, 48.

42. Dwan J. Young, "Draw Near to Him in Prayer," *Ensign,* November 1985, 91.

43. Peterson, "Dwan J. Young: Primarily Devoted to Children," 35.

44. "Primary, 1982: A Conversation with the General Primary Presidency," 48.

45. Telephone interview with Suzanne Y. Jones, 25 January 1994.

46. Telephone interview with Jeffrey Young, 1 March 1994.

47. Telephone interview with Paul Young, 22 March 1994.

48. Telephone interview with Suzanne Y. Jones, 25 January 1994.

49. Ibid.

50. Interview with Dwan J. Young, 26 May 1993.

51. Ibid.

52. Telephone interview with Thomas Young, 15 March 1994.

53. Telephone interview with Brant J. Taylor, 15 March 1994.

54. Interview with Dwan J. Young, 26 May 1993.

55. Telephone interview with Thomas Young, 15 March 1994.

56. Interview with Dwan J. Young, 26 May 1993.

57. Telephone interview with Dwan J. Young, 9 November 1994.

58. Telephone interview with Michael Young, 1 March 1994.

59. Telephone interview with Thomas Young, 15 March 1994.

60. Interview with Vauna S. Jacobsen, 5 January 1994.

61. Telephone interview with Christine Y. Knudson, 18 January 1994.

62. Ibid.

63. Telephone interview with Dwan J. Young, 9 November 1994.

Chapter Eight: Michaelene Packer Grassli

1. Michaelene P. Grassli, *What I Have Learned From Children* (Salt Lake City: Deseret Book Co., 1994), 3.

2. Telephone interview with Betty Jo N. Jepsen, 6 January 1994.

3. Telephone interview with Ruth B. Wright, 21 January 1994.

4. Except where noted, family history information was provided by Dottie M. Packer and Michaelene P. Grassli.

5. Donna Smith Packer, *On Footings from the Past: The Packers in England* (Salt Lake City: Donna Smith Packer, 1988), 378–83.

6. "An Account of the Journey to Utah Across the Plains of the First Handcart Company Led by Edmund Ellsworth, 1856," unpublished manuscript in possession of Dottie M. Packer.

7. Interview with Dottie M. Packer, 9 June 1993.

8. Interview with Michaelene P. Grassli, 25 May 1993.

9. Interview with Dottie M. Packer, 9 June 1993.

10. Gerry Avant, "Hers Is a Life of Service," *Church News,* 30 April 1988, 6.

11. Interview with Michaelene P. Grassli, 25 May 1993.

12. Sandra Stallings, "Friend to Friend," *Friend,* September 1986, 6.

13. Telephone interview with Deanne P. Kelly, 5 February 1994.

14. Telephone interview with Deanne P. Kelly, 16 November 1994.

15. Telephone interview with Dottie M. Packer, 23 March 1994.

16. Gerry Avant, "Family Supports Call of Primary Counselor," *Church News*, 3 May 1980, 6.

17. Grassli, *What I Have Learned from Children*, 85.

18. Interview with Michaelene P. Grassli, 25 May 1993.

19. Telephone interview with Michaelene P. Grassli, 9 November 1994.

20. Interview with Michaelene P. Grassli, 25 May 1993.

21. Grassli, *What I Have Learned from Children*, 51.

22. Stallings, "Friend to Friend," 6.

23. Interview with Michaelene P. Grassli, 25 May 1993.

24. Ibid.

25. Telephone interview with Deanne P. Kelly, 5 February 1994.

26. Grassli, *What I Have Learned from Children*, 3.

27. Avant, "Hers Is a Life of Service," 6–7.

28. Telephone interview with Deanne P. Kelly, 5 February 1994.

29. Grassli, *What I Have Learned from Children*, p. 80.

30. Telephone interview with Dottie M. Packer, 7 November 1994.

31. Grassli, *What I Have Learned from Children*, p. 3.

32. Telephone interview with Susan Grassli, 27 January 1994.

33. Avant, "Family Supports Call of Primary Counselor," 6.

34. Telephone interview with Betty Jo N. Jepsen, 6 January 1994.

35. Telephone interview with Susan Grassli, 27 January 1994.

36. Telephone interview with Sara G. Chugg, 24 November 1993.

37. Telephone interview with Jane Anne G. Woodhead, 28 October 1993.

38. Avant, "Family Supports Call of Primary Counselor," 6.

39. Telephone interview with Susan Grassli, 27 January 1994.

40. Ibid.

41. Written statement of Michaelene P. Grassli to Janet Peterson, 16 November 1994.

42. Telephone interview with Susan Grassli, 27 January 1994.

43. Interview with Dwan J. Young, 26 May 1993.

44. Avant, "Hers Is a Life of Service," 13.

45. Written statement of Michaelene P. Grassli to Janet Peterson, 29 March 1994.

46. Avant, "Hers Is a Life of Service," 6.

47. Interview with Michaelene P. Grassli, 25 May 1993.

48. Written statement of Michaelene P. Grassli to Janet Peterson, 4 May 1994.

49. Telephone interview with Susan Grassli, 27 January 1994.

50. Interview with Michaelene P. Grassli, 25 May 1993.

51. Ibid.

52. Telephone interview with Michaelene P. Grassli, 9 November 1994.

53. Journal entry, in possession of Michaelene P. Grassli.

54. Grassli, *What I Have Learned from Children,* 87.

55. Avant, "Family Supports Call of Primary Counselor," 6.

56. Telephone interview with Jane Anne G. Woodhead, 3 November 1993.

57. Telephone interview with Sara G. Chugg, 24 November 1993.

58. Interview with Dwan J. Young, 26 May 1993.

59. Telephone interview with Michaelene P. Grassli, 9 November 1994.

60. Ibid.

61. Interview with Michaelene P. Grassli, 25 May 1993.

62. Telephone interview with Deanne P. Kelly, 19 January 1994.

63. "A Conversation about Primary," *Ensign,* June 1988, 78.

64. Telephone interview with Michaelene P. Grassli, 9 November 1994.

65. Ibid.

66. Letter of Joan Davis to Michaelene P. Grassli, 6 October 1994, copy in possession of Janet Peterson.

67. Poem of appreciation, Kaysville Utah Crestwood Stake, 13 October 1994, copy in possession of Janet Peterson.

68. Telephone interview with Ruth B. Wright, 21 January 1994.

69. Ibid.

70. First Presidency letter, 1 August 1993, reprinted in "Church Renews Effort to Nurture Children," *Church News,* 27 November 1993, 3.

71. "Church Renews Effort to Nurture Children," 4.

72. Michaelene P. Grassli, "Teaching Our Children," First Presidency Satellite Broadcast, 23 January 1994, typescript in possession of Janet Peterson.

73. Interview with Michaelene P. Grassli, 25 May 1994.

74. Telephone interview with Kelly M. Packer, 20 February 1994.

75. Telephone interview with Michaelene P. Grassli, 9 November 1994.

76. Telephone interview with Leonard M Grassli, 24 November 1993.

77. Written statement of Michaelene P. Grassli to Janet Peterson, 29 March 1994.

78. Telephone interview with Betty Jo N. Jepsen, 6 January 1993.

79. Telephone interview with Ruth B. Wright, 21 January 1994.

80. Telephone interview with Virginia H. Pearce, 17 March 1994.

81. Ibid.

82. Telephone interview with Ruth B. Wright, 21 January 1994.

83. Telephone interview with Judy F. Edwards, 18 February 1994.

84. Telephone interview with Michaelene P. Grassli, 9 November 1994.

85. Interview with Michaelene P. Grassli, 25 May 1993.

86. Written statement of Michaelene P. Grassli to Janet Peterson, 4 May 1994.

87. Telephone interview with Jane Anne G. Woodhead, 3 November 1993.

88. Grassli, *What I Have Learned from Children,* 6.

89. Ibid., 57.

90. Telephone interview with Dottie M. Packer, 23 March 1994.

91. Written statement of Michaelene P. Grassli to Janet Peterson, 16 November 1994.

92. Telephone interview with Michaelene P. Grassli, 9 November 1994.

93. Interview with Michaelene P. Grassli, 25 May 1993.   '

Chapter Nine: Patricia Peterson Pinegar

1. Interview with Patricia P. Pinegar, 26 October 1994.

2. Letter from Laurence Peterson, original in possession of LaRene Gaunt.

3. All family history stories are from Patricia P. Pinegar's family records in her possession, a copy in possession of LaRene Gaunt.

4. Interview with Patricia P. Pinegar, 19 October 1994.

5. Letter from Laurence Peterson, original in possession of LaRene Gaunt.

6. Interview with Patricia P. Pinegar, 19 October 1994.

7. Letter from Laurelee Peterson Passey, original in possession of LaRene Gaunt.

8. Patricia P. Pinegar, "Increase in Faith," *Ensign,* May 1994, 94.

9. Letter from David Peterson, original in possession of LaRene Gaunt.

10. Julie A. Dockstader, "Nothing is deeper than 'simple faith,' a basis for her life," *Church News,* 5 November 1994, 6.

11. Telephone interview with Ed J. Pinegar, December 1994.

12. Interview with Patricia P. Pinegar, 19 October 1994.

13. Ibid.

14. Ibid.

15. Telephone interview with Ed J. Pinegar, December 1994.

16. Letter from Traci Pinegar Magleby, original in possession of LaRene Gaunt.

17. Letter from Tricia Pinegar, original in possession of LaRene Gaunt.

18. Letter from Steven Pinegar, original in possession of LaRene Gaunt.

19. Letter from Kelly Pinegar Hagemeyer, original in possession of LaRene Gaunt.

20. Letter from Brett J. Pinegar, original in possession of LaRene Gaunt.

21. Letter from Karie Pinegar Bushnell, original in possession of LaRene Gaunt.

22. Interview with Patricia P. Pinegar, 19 October 1994.

23. Telephone interview with Ed J. Pinegar, December 1994.

24. Interview with Patricia P. Pinegar, 19 October 1994.

25. Letter from Kristi Pinegar Gubler, original in possession of LaRene Gaunt.

26. Letter from Laurelee Peterson Passey, original in possession of LaRene Gaunt.

27. Letter from Karie Pinegar Bushnell, original in possession of LaRene Gaunt.

28. Dockstader, "Nothing is deeper than 'simple faith,'" *Church News,* 5 November 1994, 7.

29. Interview with Patricia P. Pinegar, 16 October 1994.

30. "New Young Women General Presidency Called," *Ensign,* May 1992, 106–7.

31. Interview with Patricia P. Pinegar, 26 October 1994.

32. Letter from Traci Pinegar Magleby, original in possession of LaRene Gaunt.

33. Interview with Patricia P. Pinegar, 26 October 1994.

34. Memo from Janette Hales Beckham to LaRene Gaunt, 16 February 1995, original in possession of LaRene Gaunt.

35. Interview with Patricia P. Pinegar, 26 October 1994.

36. Ibid.

37. Memo from Janette Hales Beckham to LaRene Gaunt, 16 February 1995, original in possession of LaRene Gaunt.

38. Patricia P. Pinegar, "Teach the Children," *Ensign,* November 1994, 78–79.

39. Letter from Susan Carol Lilywhite Warner, original in possession of LaRene Gaunt.

40. Interview with Patricia P. Pinegar, 26 October 1994.

41. Telephone interview with Ed J. Pinegar, December 1994.

42. Interview with Patricia P. Pinegar, 26 October 1994.

43. Ibid.

Index